"The Object Lessons series achieves something very close to magic: the books take ordinary—even banal—objects and animate them with a rich history of invention, political struggle, science, and popular mythology. Filled with fascinating details and conveyed in sharp, accessible prose, the books make the everyday world come to life. Be warned: once you've read a few of these, you'll start walking around your house, picking up random objects, and musing aloud: 'I wonder what the story is behind this thing?'"

Steven Johnson, author of *Where Good Ideas Come From* and *How We Got to Now*

"Object Lessons describes themselves as 'short, beautiful books,' and to that, I'll say, amen. . . . If you read enough Object Lessons books, you'll fill your head with plenty of trivia to amaze and annoy your friends and loved ones—caution recommended on pontificating on the objects surrounding you. More importantly, though . . . they inspire us to take a second look at parts of the everyday that we've taken for granted. These are not so much lessons about the objects themselves, but opportunities for self-reflection and storytelling. They remind us that we are surrounded by a wondrous world, as long as we care to look."

John Warner, *The Chicago Tribune*

The joy of the series . . . lies in encountering the various turns through which each of the authors has been put by his or her object. The object predominates, sits squarely center stage, directs the action. The object decides the genre, the chronology, and the limits of the study. Accordingly, the author has to take her cue from the *thing* she chose or that chose her. The result is a wonderfully uneven series of books, each one a *thing* unto itself."

Julian Yates, *Los Angeles Review of Books*

. . . edifying and entertaining . . . perfect for slipping in a pocket and pulling out when life is on hold."

Sarah Murdoch, *Toronto Star*

. . . a sensibility somewhere between Roland Barthes and Wes Anderson."

Simon Reynolds, **author of** *Retromania: Pop Culture's Addiction to Its Own Past*

OBJECT LESSONS

A book series about the hidden lives of ordinary things.

Series Editors:

Ian Bogost and Christopher Schaberg

Advisory Board:

Sara Ahmed, Jane Bennett, Jeffrey Jerome Cohen, Johanna Drucker, Raiford Guins, Graham Harman, renée hoogland, Pam Houston, Eileen Joy, Douglas Kahn, Daniel Miller, Esther Milne, Timothy Morton, Kathleen Stewart, Nigel Thrift, Rob Walker, Michele White.

In association with

LOYOLA UNIVERSITY NEW ORLEANS   Georgia Tech | Center for Media Studies

BOOKS IN THE SERIES

veil

RAFIA ZAKARIA

BLOOMSBURY ACADEMIC

NEW YORK • LONDON • OXFORD • NEW DELHI • SYDNEY

BLOOMSBURY ACADEMIC
Bloomsbury Publishing Inc
1385 Broadway, New York, NY 10018, USA
50 Bedford Square, London, WC1B 3DP, UK

BLOOMSBURY, BLOOMSBURY ACADEMIC and the Diana logo are trademarks
of Bloomsbury Publishing Plc

First published 2017
Reprinted by Bloomsbury Academic 2018, 2019

Cover design: Alice Marwick

Bloomsbury Publishing Inc does not have any control over, or responsibility for, any
third-party websites referred to or in this book. All internet addresses given in this
book were correct at the time of going to press. The author and publisher regret any
inconvenience caused if addresses have changed or sites have ceased to exist, but
can accept no responsibility for any such changes.

No responsibility for loss caused to any individual or organization acting on
or refraining from action as a result of the material in this publication can
be accepted by Bloomsbury or the author.

Library of Congress Cataloguing-in-Publication Data
Names: Zakaria, Rafia, 1978- author.
Title: Veil / Rafia Zakaria.
Description: New York : Bloomsbury Academic, 2017. | Includes index.
Identifiers: LCCN 2017012308 | ISBN 9781501322778 (pbk. : alk. paper) |
ISBN 9781501322785 (epub)
Subjects: LCSH: Veils–Religious aspects–Islam. | Hijab (Islamic clothing) | Muslim
women–Clothing. | Veils–Political aspects. | Veils–Social aspects.
Classification: LCC BP190.5.H44 Z35 2017 | DDC 297.5/76–dc23
LC record available at https://lccn.loc.gov/2017012308

ISBN: PB: 978-1-5013-2277-8
ePub: 978-1-5013-2278-5
ePDF: 978-1-5013-2279-2

Series: Object Lessons

Typeset by Deanta Global Publishing Services, Chennai, India
Printed and bound in the United States of America

To find out more about our authors and books visit www.bloomsbury.com
and sign up for our newsletters.

CONTENTS

INTRODUCTION

A book, I have learned, begins in the heart, germinating and sprouting long before its author—the incidental host body—even knows of its existence. So it was with this one; it began in the summer of 2011, a part of which I spent in a hospital waiting room in Karachi. My mother was sick, sliding in and out of consciousness, sometimes sedated, sometimes wracked by seizures and sometimes slipping away. Time, per the rules of institution, was spliced into ten-minute portions that I was permitted to spend with her in the Special Care Unit. The rest of it, a recurring forty-eight minutes (sans the one each it took to walk to and from the sanctuary of the especially ailing), was waiting.

Hospital waiting rooms and their inhabitants are special cases because of what brings them together. The utilitarian frugality of their design, the worn furniture that bears witness to surreal pairings of hope and horror, walls that will support the deliverance of deadly news to changing but predictable recipients, combine to form a wary and literal cusp between life and death. The room I was in stayed true to these general parameters: a windowless rectangle, its longer walls were taken up by two long couches flush against them; the cushions were navy blue and could not be removed. People do strange things when waiting for news—perhaps removing couch cushions is one of them. The short wall held a shorter couch of similar type, a cushion-less spot in the middle functioning as a sort of table, piled with well-thumbed magazines people may remember from another era before they were occupied with questions of life and death. As it is in much of the world, caregiving and concern, even when it is for the ailing and the almost dying, falls mostly to women. It was for this reason that the numbers of men and women in the waiting room that summer were about equal.

Equality in numbers, however, does not mean equality in power, the avowed entitlement over public space that is continually exerted by men all over the world. This could be seen in the de facto gender arrangement of the room. The women, alone or in pairs, huddled with other women along one side of the room, trying to insure via their proximity to each other that a man would not deign to sit next to them. If empty space was unavoidable, temporary fortifications of plastic bags, purses, duffel bags, newspapers, bags of fruit or fried samosas, could be erected. If a man did sit down next to you, your existing line of defense could be further augmented, but the defeat was visible. Men feel entitled to sit, their dominion a threat even amid the already heavy emotional burdens borne by everyone in the room.

It was in these tense, stressful moments that I encountered a woman whose mien and manner would instigate this inquiry. She was fully veiled, her entire body encased in a long brown polyester overcoat. Her face, neck, and shoulders were covered with a brown veil that matched her coat, the only visible segment of her body a generous slit revealing a portion of forehead and eyes. The eyes were notable, scanning and absorbing and looking—not simply at the other women who sat meekly praying or shooting darting, hesitant glances at each other, but also at the men in the room. When a man entered, or simply sat staring, legs akimbo on the opposite side of the room, the woman silently, or sometimes even while speaking loudly on a cell phone, stared back.

Staring back at a man, or at groups of men, is a significant act in Pakistan. If a woman who is unveiled (her face visible) stares back it suggests romantic interest. Entire love affairs are built on a man believing a woman is romantically interested simply because she returns his glance instead of staring away. The consequence for most women is a deliberate and constant turning away, of being but not looking, simply to avoid the cost of looking, the suggestion of whetting the sexual and romantic appetites of the men nearby. This woman, however, was not looking away. Her face shielded and her identity not amenable to the general public of the waiting room, she stared back, long and hard, until one man, then another and many more were forced to look away.

She didn't practice any of the other tricks of subterfuge for survival that are used by women trying to survive and thrive in a male-dominated public space. With her billowing coat settling down around her every time she sat down, she did not bother to erect fortifications or seem to worry about what sort of possibly lecherous, potentially harassing man sat next to her. While other women busied themselves reading or talking among themselves in low voices, this woman refused to abridge her presence. When she entered the room she did not shrink and skulk into a shadow. When she spoke on her cellphone (and she did this quite often), it was at a male-like volume—a volume used by women only in private settings where they are untrammeled by the challenge of constituting the existing but invisible.

My mother's sojourn in Special Care lasted for nearly a week. For five of these days, my presence in the waiting room coincided with that of the fully veiled woman. In the initial days, perhaps made because of the shock and sudden nature of my mother's hospitalization, I arrived at the waiting room dressed as I ordinarily did. I wore a shalwar kamiz, the loose tunic and bottoms that are customary in Pakistan. I also wore a scarf or dupatta that duly wrapped around my chest. Nearly all of my body save my hair, face, and neck was covered. I considered this adequate.

It was not. I learned after the first day that the direction of my gaze was constantly and duly followed. If I touched my hair, it was noticed; if I talked to a cousin or to anyone else who came to visit and inquire, the conversations were listened to without attempt at concealment. My conversations, the book I tried to read, my body when I got up and my choice of place when I sat down, all were subject to the ever-present, ever-staring men. By the second day I wound my scarf around myself a bit tighter. On the third day onward, I was covering my hair with the scarf and on the final day I was wishing I had a full veil just like the one the woman wore.

As a writer and an activist, I am acutely aware of the prismatic symbolism of the veil, reflecting in turn the political and social beliefs of a society, its dimensions connected to where a culture or a woman situates herself on the spectrum of religious faith and secular belief. These are contentious debates, not least ones in which Muslim women, those that wear the veil and those that do not, are pinned and pushed into the necessity of choice, of ratifying their own decisions about one or the other thesis concerning its rightness or wrongness. The hefty burdens of these debates, many of which have been articulated, pushed and pandered by men (who duly reward the women who pick their sides with gracious pats on the back, paeans to courage or moral purity) have obscured novel considerations of the veil as object. In this sense, the aesthetics of the veil, tied as they are to alter the physical spaces in which they are worn, to construct a simultaneous occasion of presence and non-presence, being and non-being, are left untouched.

It is also a personal inquiry, an investigation of my own relationship to the veil. In presenting fragments from my own life in which the veil has figured significantly, I hope to take you the reader on a journey of the changing self, eroded or enriched by the passage of time, and describe how this self stands in relation to a particular physical object. At different times in my life, I have worn the veil, abandoned the veil,

wished for the veil, championed the veil . . . and in all of them
[I have been earnest in my attunement toward it and relation to
it based on particularities of person and politics and context.]
In relaying this journey, I hope to reveal not some incipient
truth about the veil itself, but rather its multidimensionality
not simply as the moral or political indicator to which it
is relegated but rather as a facet of life that transforms and
reforms during its course.

We live in a world where visibility signifies power and
control. In our everyday lives we seek to see and be seen,
considering our physical reality and its dimensions of race
and gender a big portion of our identity as people. Large parts
of our days are devoted to insuring we look a certain way,
that we project a certain sort of physical reality. The distance
that this reality marks between ideal types, what we wish to
be, how we wish to be, is often a source of great concern and
perturbation. For women especially, the physical realities of
their bodies exert undue influence on the more amorphous
qualities and attitudes that they are believed to possess.

With the arrival and embrace of social media platforms
and the ubiquity of virtual engagement, the practice and
prominence of visibility has extended even farther. If we were
only visible in a limited physical sense before the arrival of
the internet, its colonization of our lives has turned visibility
into a virtue. Through a torrent of social media platforms,
some like Instagram devoted entirely and particularly to what
is visually real, we produce and consume images of others.
Central to our consumption is the idea that the visible is

good, and that more visibility is a net positive, its constant accruals a sort of progress on the road of greater projections of self. Selfies—pictures of ourselves taken by ourselves and usually constituting only the face—are essential instruments to this idea of visibility as good and powerful. We generate scores of them every day and share them with friends and strangers, and each time we do, we reiterate the premise that the *I* in our identities accords in some rough equivalent with our visible selves, or at least in the curated versions of our physical selves we present on social media.

The irony of our collective championing of visibility is that it seems to function in dogged disregard of the fact that invisibility, even if we may want it, is increasingly impossible. The GPS on our iPhones can geo-locate our Instagram photos; checking into various places via Foursquare allows data to be collected for marketing purposes; connecting to public Wi-Fi at restaurants, airports, and other places reveals information not simply regarding location but on everything from food preferences to friends, purchases, and more. Beyond virtual means, cameras—present in nearly every cubby and corner of urban environments—further monitor the activities of our physical selves. At the same time, the ease of use promised by GPS systems, the supposed safety they add to our everyday lives, is so seductive that, despite ominous warnings by data scientists and surveillance experts, most consumers remain largely unconcerned by or oblivious to its dangers. The precept that visibility is good, that the tracking of our digital footprint and even our physical self is a positive addition to our lives, is so entrenched that few are willing to change behavior even against the loss of privacy, the threat of being constantly watched, tracked and recorded.

It is no wonder then that the veil surprises, perturbs and disconcerts: (its power as an object bears the potential of obliterating in the instance of its use the very visibility whose dogged pursuit seems to take up so much time.) The power and provocation of the veil cannot be appreciated without considering the concomitant rise in the value of visibility that has occurred in recent years. To appreciate the depth of this development, consider the fact that even as late as the 1600s, ordinary people did not have access to mirrors and so had little idea of what they looked like. Photography, at least in the sense of being available to all, was at least a hundred years into to the future. The very wealthy could commission portraits and afford mirrors, but beyond this, the consciousness of one's physical self and the projection of this self out to others were not as ubiquitous as is today.

Today a fully veiled woman sitting at an airport terminal in London represents a different amalgamation of identity indicators than one who isn't. The digital and physical identity of an unveiled woman sitting next to her coalesce and cohere; her physical identity, her *face*, can be verified by any one of the many cameras in the terminal. Similarly, her digital identity can be picked up by the signals sent by her phone to cellular phone towers if she checks into the terminal via Facebook, posts a picture of her snack on Instagram. In the case of the first woman physical identity—at least in the sense visible to cameras—may be unverifiable. Digital identity, however, can still reveal who she is and what her preferences may be based on her digital behavior. The crucial difference is that save biometric functions or touch identification, her digital identity—because it exists apart from her camouflaged physical reality—can be the exactly the same as that of another person with the simple transference of whichever mobile or electronic device she is using.

The veil as object is central to this attempt at elusion. Its function in this case, to eliminate physicality from the identity equation, enables the creation of a third state of being, a limbo between existence and non-existence where either can be actualized but neither really is. The removal of the veil permits in this sense, a more complete being, a meeting of the digital and the physical. A continued wearing of the veil similarly suggests a suspension where the two do not meet.

For me, this is also a convenient culmination of metaphor: The veiled woman whose identity is not visible, yet who can see and perceive and process and exist digitally, logging locations and preferences, is similar to the condition of my mother and other patients in the Special Care Unit, where I first encountered the impetus for this book. Just as these patients can be described conversely as struggling to live or easing into death, the power of the veil as an object is its segregation of reality and identity into separate parts. The veiled woman both *is* and *is* not, the veil itself in this case very much an option, and the possibilities and constraints of availing it are the subject of this book.

1 SUBMISSION

I wore the full-face veil for the first time on my wedding day. I was eighteen years old and I had never worn it before. In Pakistani Muslim tradition, this was the day of the ceremonial giving away of the bride, the day I was to say goodbye to my family (theatrically and before an audience of a few hundred) and go off to be with my husband and his family. The fabric I had chosen over a year before for my wedding dress had been selected for hue and sheen—a fiery red-orange—and it was utterly opaque. I could see nothing. For navigation, I had the assistance of two younger cousins, unveiled and full of giggles. It was September in Karachi, I was pouring sweat and also blind.

The story of how I ended up fully veiled and a bride did not begin that day. The skein connecting it to incidents past could be reeled back to an event a few years earlier, one that had led me to begin wearing the half-veil or the headscarf. Fifteen then, I was a student at an all-girls school that prided itself in being almost entirely free of the contaminating male presence, whose very existence made veils necessary in the first place. The hundreds of girls that were students there were instructed almost entirely by women. From the time we were six years old and began first grade to the time we were seventeen and graduated eleventh, it was women, women and all women. At five past eight every morning, the gates of the school would be locked and the man-free day would begin. The only men left inside were the very poor ones that the school employed, who mopped the halls, set up the nets for games of volleyball behind our high walls, or guarded the gates. The fact that they were poor seemed to cancel out their masculinity.

There were no men at school and so within its walls there were no veils, the walls and seclusion functioning as its own sort of full veil. This changed when school hours ended; when the gates were opened in the afternoon many girls were quick to put on a head scarf, and some, notably fewer, even a full-face veil. The rest of us took the small distance from our school, where we were kept from the male presence, to the cars that took us home, to attract as much male attention as we could. Meaningful glances, wordless flirting, and eventually telephone numbers were all exchanged surreptitiously. A boys' school was not far away, and the boys came in droves— to see and, if they were more ambitious, to seduce. It was a window of opportunity for young love.

It was that December that our tenth-grade class, of 35 sixteen-year-old girls, decided to plan a picnic. Central to the excursion was the hefty battalion of chaperones who would accompany us, six or seven matronly teachers who had taught us Physics or Chemistry or Mathematics and could be convinced to add another day to their workweek for the promise of a bit of sun and sea. To insure that the all-girl environment of the school could be replicated on the picnic, we would be headed to a private beach, where we would spend the day at a private beach house, all of it guarded by armed private guards at the entrance and exit. Because of this, we could be unveiled if fully clothed, out in the open but still unseen, still out of the reach of men. ✦

The day of the picnic came, spirits were high and laughter was everywhere. There was no one at all on the empty stretch of private beach except our group of girls and chaperones. They sat in a line watching us, their own heads covered against the sun or by habit while we giggled and squealed at the shoreline—December is the only month in which Karachi's heavy heat abates but the breeze, the sun, and the ocean, despite their proximity, were not usually available to us. Our school building, dating all the way back to 1905, sat in the fetid heart of a polluted downtown, the air we breathed choked up with the fumes of buses and cars. In studies it was cited as the most polluted point of a very polluted city. Freed from this miasma, we drank fitfully of the freedom, the lack of walls, and gates, the veils that stood between us, the natural and unnatural barriers that made up our lives.

It was in the midst of this that the boys came. They had been unable to come from the land, its single route blocked off by the guards, and so they came from the sea. There they were in a speedboat that appeared on the horizon, four or five of them dark haired and excited against a blue sun-drenched horizon. As we watched, the boat they were in came closer and closer, until their faces and their voices and their maleness was visible to all. Then, they began to call out my name. They did it once, and then again after they brought the boat to the shore, after they dragged it to an adjoining house, and after they took up spots in its front porch. They could see everything.

The chaperones were terrified. It was their worst nightmare: exposed girls on an exposed beach beset by unknown men. They called out to us to come back up the beach, to come closer to them, to hide ourselves. With the appearance of men, even boys, our visibility was a problem. Once we had been evacuated from the beach, new instructions were issued; we had to stay close as possible to the chaperones, as far away as possible from the boys. There was an air of doom to it all; a terrible thing had happened, the fun was over. Many promises had been made to the parents that had permitted their daughters to go and now those promises had been broken.

We did not leave immediately. We stayed long enough for the boys to call out my name a few more times, for several of my classmates to hear it and for them to tell others. We were raised to be good girls and most were better girls and eager to prove it by emphasizing my complicity. By the time we all packed up for the long morose ride back to school, there were also accusing glances from the teachers. Glib and meaningful, they all said the same thing: "I know you had a part in this." I was in trouble. The coastal road connected us back to the highway, which led us back into the city, to the safety of the walled school that veiled us from the outside. My crime was clear: I had somehow inspired a collective, non-consensual unveiling of those that did not wish it.

Not long after the picnic, I began to wear the headscarf. There had been much fallout in its aftermath; my mother was summoned to school for solemn discussions. The smug and indignant chaperones, spinsters all, had hinted at expulsion, fueled by the certainty of my immorality, the horror of what had happened.

I was not expelled, since there was no proof and I refused to supply it. To save myself, I stolidly stuck to denial. I did not know who the boys were; I had no idea why or how they screamed my name. I was certain that some of the girls were inflating their stories.

It was a lie, but a self-preserving one. I could not admit that I knew the boys, or at least the one of them that had slipped me his phone number as I walked out from school one day. Nor could I say that I had talked to him several times on the phone and that he had asked to meet every one of those times. Every time, I had told him it was impossible, that I was kept behind wall and key, never alone or unwatched. Then, one day I had mentioned the picnic, half-knowingly but assured of the fact that he would not be able to penetrate the defenses of guards and cordons. I had underestimated his persistence, his belief in the possibility of a rendezvous.

Men = Crazy

Even though I was not expelled or suspended, I faced banishment of another sort. In the delicate moral ecosystem of our classroom of sixteen-year-old girls, I had ceded space to a premature male invasion, an impermissible one. We inhabited a climate in which the precariousness of our condition, our veiled yet unveiled state behind the sheltering walls of our school, was constantly and consistently under-scored. There were threats and warnings and prognostications of how awful that world, that world where men dominated, where their gaze was omnipresent was a harsh one. We were to relish this time of sequestered freedom. I had disrespected it and I deserved no mercy.

To survive that last year of school, I needed a visible act of contrition—and so I chose the headscarf. There was a redundancy to it that could have been comical: I was choosing to be additionally veiled in an environment that was, owing to its sequestration, already veiled and hidden away. But I was suffering the long and deep pangs of teenage exclusion; there was no humor in it for me. Luckily and eventually there was also some respite. My one-and-a-half-times veiled (once by the sequestered school and another half by the headscarf), newly pious self appeared sufficiently recalcitrant. My betrayal, if not forgotten, was forgiven. I was slowly and again included in conversations, in potlucks arranged for recess, in all the little joys of our sequestered world.

I had been a rebel, and then I became a conformist—and I discovered that it was lovely and even addictive. There were fewer secrets and less intrigue. All suffering, particularly the sort of imposed by men, was shared suffering; there were loads of camaraderie and a sense of shared identity. We were all girls in it together against a male world that wanted to claim us. Being walled-in at school, to December picnic, to the half veil and then, a year or so later, the full veil were all steps on a path, I can see it now—but the ultimate destination of course was unknown to me then. I knew, however, that it implicated connections between all of this: dots drawn between veiling, sequestering, men, submission and rebellion. There was strategy in it and manipulation, some instinctual and not quite explicit understanding of what it meant to belong and how belonging could be accomplished, in this case via an object, a headscarf and then a veil.

Veiled meanings

The full-veiled self that arrived at my wedding that September in Karachi was in some part high on the same drug of approval and approbation. The issue of choice, Muslim women's choices as a collective, their choices surrounding arranged marriages, and of course and centrally the choices concerning veiling and unveiling, are the matter of much and heated debate. Entire legislative sessions in several countries have been devoted to the issue, not to mention hundreds of pages of precedent-twisting judicial decisions that come down on either side of this vexing issue. It is a difficult project, however, and one so heavy with the weight of its political implications. Separating the threads of any dense woven fabric is a daunting task and so of course is the case here, even when the decision and its dimensions were my very own.

I was not forced to marry, or even persuaded to marry; but I was, at a very young age, whose significance was emphasized by all those who posed the choice to me, presented with the opportunity. I was sixteen and I said yes to the proposal and to marrying the man I had been introduced to at my grandmother's house six months earlier. We had not spoken for longer than a few minutes, and even then I had known that there was something momentous about the occasion. In the nearly all-female environment (save young male cousins) of my grandmother's house, there had been the sudden and inexplicable presence of a man. Accustomed to being sent upstairs or away when such visitors appeared, the very arrangement of the event was indicative. The proposal itself came months later, after many more relatives had been involved, many fervent discussions held as my mother grilled her sisters who knew his mother. Visits by his parents, discussions about him all generally proceeding and persisting like a growing chorus in the background of my life. That life, however, also continued—school and its incipient dramatics, the stress of this or that test, the inequities of teachers I didn't like, the coveting of freedoms I didn't have.

Unlike so much else in Pakistan that relies centrally on ritual, the moment I was asked whether I agreed to the marriage was simple and unassuming. We, my parents, my brother, and I, had just returned from a wedding. I was still in the finery I had been permitted for the occasion. A long burgundy velvet tunic, the gold thread embroidery at its neck cut carefully from an old one that had belonged to my mother, tradition and beauty given new life via a talented and temperamental tailor. I was sitting on the edge of my bed, the glass-topped table in front of me covered with schoolbooks, behind me the three-mirrored dressing table that had belonged to an aunt. The two side mirrors were hinged to the larger one and could be turned so that you could get a good look at the back of your head. It was useful for French braids or if you wanted to be surrounded by endless, infinitely regressing images of yourself.

I said yes. I was asked if I was sure and I insisted I was. That was the extent of the conversation. My parents seemed surprised and perhaps they really were. Apart from the very recent turn toward the headscarf, a fad that had flummoxed rather than flattered them, I had been the most predictably rebellious and argumentative of their offspring. I had, in the past and as a young child, defied the idea of marriage, castigated my mother's domesticity and insisted I would not marry at all. Riding the initial, heady waves of pubescent hormones I had denounced all that was part of my mother's life: the raising of children, the cooking of meals, the waiting for the husband. In retrospect, it seems of course both predictable and banal, the parameters of what I thought wrong, the kitchen chores I skirted, the entirely usual ways

Her Life ≠ Mom's Life ✱

in which I sought to convince <u>myself that my life would not</u> <u>be my mother's life.</u>

Scary veils and pretty veils

American wedding

The ceremonial wedding gown, often accompanied by the veil, is a centerpiece of nuptials in many cultures. Even in the United States and other Western countries, the drama surrounding the selection of the dress, its price and particulars, its cut and crease, who pays for it and who gets to veto it are milestones in the run-up to a couple's nuptials. The popularity of the television show *Say Yes to the Dress*, now in its fourteenth season, can be considered a rough testament that even in cultures where ritual and tradition are never usually enough to alter decisions to dictate the denouement of events or selections of spouses, they retain a level of importance. The amalgamated drama of the bride's big day, the relatives varying opinions and expectations, tight budgets and amorphous ones, first-time brides versus grandmothers marrying later in life all make for good television. Even the arguably un-feminist obsession with how the bride as the centerpiece of the day is cast to the side, the veritable obsession with female physicality, too-big or too-small hips and bosoms, the blessedness of camouflage accomplished by the architecture of fabrics, all deemed permissible within this particular context. <u>The American</u> wedding is also the only place that the full-face veil makes an appearance without its usual attachments of sinister suspicions; the veiled bride is considered neither repressed nor suffering, not a terrorist in hiding nor a woman marking her resistance against visibility by pursuit of its dogged opposite. Rather, this veiled bride is sweet and pure, not only permissible but ideal.

The comparison is necessary because it captures the benign lack of consideration I attached to the full-face veil or that I was to wear it for a time at the wedding reception. And while I may have been like an American bride in that I spent little time considering the veil or my wearing of it, I was dramatically different in other ways. Selecting an extremely expensive dress at sixteen felt not like the siren of freedom abridged but rather more like an achievement of empowered personhood. Suddenly, I had a say in serious details involving large expenditures; a rather intoxicating feeling for one used at best to considering selections of books or friends of ice-cream flavors. What I remember from those days leading up to the wedding was the sheer variety of the choices and (in retrospect) the somewhat arbitrary basis on which I made them.

My husband-to-be (we were now permitted phone conversations in light of our fast-approaching coupledom) asked whether I would deign to live in the apartment he already lived in. The other option was to move to a new apartment closer to his work and the city and not quite so suburban (which I would later learn also means desolate). I hedged; I had lived in the same house and in the same city all of my life, but I was a teenager very committed to appearing worldly. So

I hedged and hedged and when pressed said that we could decide together once I got there. I did not know about leases, the requirements to fulfill their terms. It seemed like a very clever solution.

The choices others put before me were at least seemingly of less import: what sort of luggage did I want? (!) I had never been on a plane or purchased anything more than my school backpack. Clever as I was, I insisted upon green suitcases, tough plastic ones since they don't lose their shape. From my mother-in-law-to-be there were inquiries about my favorite perfume, my brand of cosmetics, what color bedding, what sort of towels, what brand of china. I perused a few dated issues of *Vogue* and came up with responses to all that, too. I felt like I was proceeding at a successful clip to becoming a wife.

Overwhelmed by these choices, I did not notice the choices that were *not* offered. My husband-to-be, who was so graciously asking my opinion of various apartments or suburbs I had never seen, did not ask where I would like to go to college. My parents, arranging the details of the wedding, the extensive menus for three days of celebrations, did not ask if I wanted a smaller wedding, something fewer than the five hundred people. Like most brides in Pakistan then, I knew only some of the people at my wedding and had less of an idea of what sort of college, apartment, or husband awaited me at the other side of the wedding. Too young to be really worried and too overwhelmed to inquire after details, I dressed up in my wedding gown, was primped and coiffed by friends and family, was laden with the ceremonial gifts

of jewelry from his parents and mine and waited. The bride
must arrive last.

Unveiling and tradition

The veiling did not take place until I had arrived at the venue.
To get there, I had to be wrapped in a large white piece of
cloth. This was not due to tradition but an effort at crime
prevention and the reality that in increasingly lawless Karachi,
a bride meant jewelry and jewelry signified an opportunity for
robbery. For my father, at least, this was a pressing concern and
hence the huge white cloth. It felt already late when my father's
cousin, entrusted with the task of transporting the bride to the
groom, finally arrived. And so, in a terrible hurry to get to my
wedding, I was wrapped up and planted in the front passenger
seat of a Toyota hatchback. I had never been in a car driven by
this relative before. He braked suddenly and often, and each
time I—wearing several yards of silk wrapped in complicated
layers all around me, laden with several pounds of gold—
lurched forward nearly into the dashboard.

My mother was waiting when I got there, as were the
cousins who would be escorting me down the long red
carpet, at the end of which and on a dais, my groom awaited.
The veil was necessary for the ritual that would be performed
once the groom and I were seated. My aunt, the common
relative—his aunt by marriage, mine by blood—would raise
the veil. In her hand she would hold a mirror, an antique

piece that belonged to my maternal grandmother. On our wedding day, the groom and I would first see each other in this mirror, in reflection, such that all the evil eyes directed at us would be warded off.

When I look at pictures of the moment now, the veil seems terribly long, made even longer in the photograph by the fact that my head is bowing downward. It could not but have been so; the fabric was heavy, bordered with huge pieces of gold lacework weighing several pounds. I wanted to, but I could not lift my head up. I also learned that when I looked down I could, at least in some small way, see the ground that I was walking on. It was better to see a little than to be completely blind.

There is a picture also of the unveiling. In it you can see my aunt's arm as it holds the mirror; she had worn pink silk that day and she holds the mirror as best as she can between our faces. My veil has been lifted and I can be seen. My husband peers into the mirror following the instruction. I do not remember looking into it or finding him there, but as traditions go, I am sure I pretended to look. I knew that the bride is not supposed to say anything at all at that moment. The groom duly exclaimed at the beauty of the bride, hidden from others, so that he would be the very first to see.

The veil as object

I trace the moment of my veiled entrance at my wedding to the ostracism I faced at that school picnic at the beach to provoke the literal question that has been at the center of my own grappling with the veil in particular, and the nature of choices in general. Are our choices, represented by the literal actions we take, the physical picking up of an object such as the veil and its putting on, or at these snapshots of decisions culminations of an ever larger and more involved webs of considerations—a previous experience, a parent's love, a lover's command, a friend's insistence whose collective congruence is sometimes reflected in what we wear or how we choose to appear? Decisions in this sense have a genealogy that, like all genealogies, has a complexity of content, an innate and obstinate resistance to being synthesized to just one thing. As with all things, we see only the visible, but what we see is not the sum total of what is.

Similarly, moments of submission and rebellion cannot be distilled into the embrace or disavowal of objects. Coercion and constraints, force and rebellion, can undoubtedly use objects to exact their ends, but the simple attachment of these to the absence or presence of choice is not simply reductive; it is destructive, unconcerned with an object's inherent possibility, its multidimensionality. The moral architecture of our decisions is complicated and I present this investigation of my own here to reveal not its universality but to suggest the necessity of a sort of structure that reveals the complexity of the decisions themselves.

Many of my friends who had been present at the picnic attended my wedding. They were, like many of my teachers, surprised that I would be the first among us to be married.

My instances of past rebellion had suggested to them that I would choose a different path from that of the veiled and jeweled teenage bride. The conversations with our younger selves are too weighted in favor of our present selves to bear many truths. I look back at the pictures, at the veil, at the mirror in whose reflection I never saw what I was supposed to see. I can remember only a feverish and forceful wish to show everyone that I was good and bold, obedient and independent. Unveiled for the rest of the reception, I talked loudly, laughed openly, and flung off all semblances of the demure. I was done with the good and obedient, I thought; I now had license to be bold and independent.

2 PURITY, NECESSITY, UNITY

My grandmother liked to visit a market that was very far from our house and near where she and my grandfather lived before I was born. The market was not like the brightly lit shops that I visited with my mother. Its lanes and corridors were open to the sky even though little light shone through the cloth canopies that stretched from the roofs of one stall to another. The stalls themselves were narrow and cavernous and most times one did not go inside but lingered near the mouth. A man usually sat there. There was no browsing; instead an assistant, always a boy and usually not much older than my four or five years at the time, would disappear into the recesses of the store and bring out whatever it was we were in the market for. Sometimes, if we were going to make a more substantial purchase, he would fetch us glass bottler of Coca-Cola with neat white straws standing at attention. I would look at my grandmother and if she nodded yes, I would drink it.

I have another memory of those trips to the bazaar. My grandmother, who still wore a sari, would on her visits to this bazar drape a long white chador around herself. Even if the sun sat high in the sky and my hand sweaty in hers, she would wear this large white cloth, her entire body enveloped within it. Sometimes, when the crowds were particularly heavy and men jostled close to us, she would drape the cloth around her face, not just her head and body. She held it in place by holding its edge in her mouth.

It was on one of these crowded days when I was walking beside her, my sweaty hand in hers, looking closely at the ground when I felt something I had never felt before. Suddenly, I felt a hand creep around my waist and pull me in the opposite direction. I resisted and the hand slipped and grabbed my behind. I think I made a small scream but I do not remember my grandmother stopping or even noticing. I never saw who it was that touched me. I remember looking up at my grandmother, all enveloped in white, all covered up, and wished I could crawl insider her veil. I do not know if I told my mother what happened, but I never went to that market with my grandmother again.

Karachi is not a very green city. Water is scarce and almost never comes in through the government water pipes. Parks, sometimes green when they are inaugurated or if they happen to be within eyeshot of powerful politicians, usually whither to dusty brown as the mostly hot months exact their lushness from them. It is perhaps for just this reason that green spaces, when they exist, are so notable, spots of verdant respite amid the dust and smog of a city of too many thirsty people. One such spot, an island really in the midst of a busy boulevard, is located near a major intersection. No larger than perhaps a thousand square feet, it features green grass, a protuberance of pink and red bougainvillea and hibiscus, terracotta pots of other flowers, and a few fledgling palm trees. Among the nonliving inhabitants of this spot, around which traffic in large choking torrents and spurting fumes of fury stops and starts constantly, are a stone bench and a small windowless room with a door. This is the pump room, which holds the means by which the city's main water line supposedly pumps water into the neighboring areas.

The little green island is circled by buildings of greater height, six and ten story structures housing stuffy offices and at least in one case, a privately run dental clinic. It was from a window in one of these clinics that one of my cousins reported seeing the following incident. At around three in the afternoon, when the heat of the city lulls people into a sort of heat-bred catatonia and traffic thins by a hair or two, a woman appeared clad in a black burka and a full veil. By herself, she sat on the bench, an oddity enjoying the grass and the flowers. Not long after, a man appeared and sat down next to her, leaving just a bit of distance between them.

From the third floor where my cousin watched them, a conversation was taking place. What was said and told and considered, could not of course be heard. What could be seen was that after a time, the man moved a bit closer to the woman. They continued to talk, albeit sporadically and then while staring straight ahead, the man put an arm around the woman. More minutes passed and a few more words appeared to have been said. Then the woman, who was even until then fully veiled, removed the portion of the veil that covered her nose and mouth. Her face could now be seen.

It was what happened next that shocked my cousin. The woman got up by herself and walked across the tiny grassy patch the where the yellow-painted pump room stood. From her purse she removed a key and undid the padlock to the pump room and went inside. The man stayed seated on the bench for a bit, shooting the heavy breeze, consuming fitful breaths of the smog-laden spot. Then he too got up, walked to the pump room and went inside. About twenty minutes later, he reappeared, taking quick steps and crossing the island into the throng on the streets surrounding the boulevard. He seemed no longer interested in or arrested by the verdant greenery. Another five minutes passed and she emerged, fully veiled again and similarly hurried. Both were lost to the crowds of Karachi.

Prostitutes are often fully veiled in Karachi. Many such burka-clad women are known to frequent busy bus stops where they can whisper to clients and quickly clasp a strange man's hand from underneath the all-covering burka, their intention and proposition clear to all parties. In a Muslim country (and fully veiled prostitutes are said to be common in many) the equation of being fully veiled with being morally pure is the sort of reductionism that begs to be co-opted. As varying oppressive regimes, from supposedly democratic Iran to the profligate monarchy of Saudi Arabia, impose the veil as a requirement, insisting that good and pure women are the ones that are completely covered, responses such as these call their bluff. The veil then serves as an armor of unassailable moral goodness that shockingly provides cover to women to make independent moral choices that may not otherwise be culturally or religiously acceptable.

The anonymity of the veil also has a role in the equation. One afternoon in Karachi, some family members and I were in the lobby of a famous five-star hotel, one of the most elite destinations in the city. In the marble lobby lit with chandeliers we sat down at the only sofa that was unoccupied. We were waiting for someone and the air-conditioned lobby of the hotel provided the sort of cool reprieve for which we had been longing. Grateful to have found a place to sit at all, we did not notice the couple that was seated at an adjacent sofa. In their early twenties, they sat next to each other and seemed perturbed that we had chosen to sit so close to them. The woman was again wearing a full burka, her veil lifted to show only her face. The man was dressed casually in khakis and a button-down shirt. They spoke in awkward bursts of sentences, all of which suggested that this was a date, likely one arranged (as in not uncommon in Pakistan) after a long flirtation via texts or social media.

In the enforced proximity of urban life, we all sat there, brought together by our desire to enjoy free air-conditioning in Karachi. The girl kept furtively scanning the room, toying with the edge of her veil. If someone she knew were to enter the lobby, she could and likely would cover up her face in an instant, retreating into the anonymity that would leave this encounter with the man who was not her husband null and void, incurring no cost at all on the unforgiving moral calculations by which Pakistan measures the moral worth of women. No one she knew ever did show up, but our proximity (even though we were both women) seemed to have added too much risk to this already risky rendezvous. Fifteen minutes or so after we arrived, the girl pulled the veil back over her face, got up and left, her heeled shoes clacking on the marble floor under the hem of her burka. Her beau, smiling and giddy, left not long after. In-person meetings are always awkward; they probably resumed and returned to the more comfortable medium of Skype and texts. Yet functioning somewhat like the easily assumed anonymity of those mediums, the veil allowed her to appear and disappear whenever she wished and wherever she was.

Not Muslim enough

The first man to tell me that I was an incomplete or inadequate Muslim because I did not veil myself was not himself a Muslim. It happened in the first several days of a class I took at the Southern Baptist College where I had been enrolled by my husband, as my continuing education was a part of the arrangement of our marriage. I was new to the United States, newer still to my understanding of the spectrum of religious denominations that constitute the American religious land-scape. It was spring and as homage to the season the instructor was holding class outside on the lawns that had once been part of a large plantation. We were spliced into little groups, meant probably to encourage exchange and conversation. I cannot remember now whether the particular subject of religion was allotted or whether it intruded, but it came up and instigated the sort of memorable small and destructive fires that such discussions have the capacity to do.

Our conversation was simple enough: I told him I was Muslim and from Pakistan. He smiled and told me this was not possible because Muslim women are required to wear a veil and I was unveiled. I remember being shocked, and as is the unfortunate curse of unforeseen moments, speechless. There were good reasons for my particular surprise. The college was almost entirely white and in the sea of whiteness were the two of us, this man and I, having an unpleasant exchange. He was Native American, and an older student; I was Pakistani and a married woman. We were both not the usual students, but this did not provide any kind of camaraderie or filial feeling. I remember telling him that he had no idea what he was talking about, that veiling was not a requirement of faith, that I had never veiled and that most women in Pakistan did not wear full-face veils and that all of them were indeed Muslim.

He smiled glibly through the whole thing—or at least that is what I remember of the incident. The slight had been sudden and sharp and expertly delivered and my defensiveness was gratifying. Here was a man telling me that I was inadequately Muslim simply because I did not fulfill his idea, his very visual idea of what a Muslim woman was supposed to be. The material of that conversation would constitute "What I could have said" and "What I should have said" for many years to come—sharp retorts whose razor edges would have wiped the smile off the man's face, freeing me of the weight of being a less than adequate Muslim, and one who was merely visibly so.

The truth regarding Muslim women and veils, non-Muslims (and many Muslims) assume, must be written up in divine doctrine, availed by an index search or a chat with a scholar then taken home to be digested, and for the truly devoted practiced. This is not so. True to the nature of all truths, rather than the particularity of this one, the reality is far more vexing. Yet the valuation or prescription of the veil as a verifiable object has continued to be rooted in its supposed religious necessity, its "requiredness" as an article of faith. For this very reason, and based perhaps on the novelty of feminist historiography within Islam (and in general), the veil debate continues to be fought with the implements of contesting verses and Hadith, or sayings of the Prophet Muhammad.[1] The two—verses of the Holy Quran and the Hadith—make up the divine sources of Islamic law.

There are no verses in the Holy Quran itself that specifically prescribe the veil for all women. As can be expected, for those that believe in the centrality of the veil as a tenet of religious practice, even the above statement is a contentious one—since the literal absence of a prescription must not be molded, in their opinion, into its invalidity. So goes the battle regarding the veil, with soldiers on either side prodded into greater, more vehement hostility which in turn is capitalized on by both repressive governments that enforce its wearing and supposedly liberal ones that ban its use.

Instead of focusing on the whether Chapter 24, Verse 30-31 of the Holy Quran—which instructs both men and women to lower their gazes and guard their private parts, and whose translation and interpretation is challenged by feminists—I would like instead to consider the rift that the debate itself has birthed among Muslim feminists. The iterations of this rift has divided friends and created enemies, not to mention imposing a measuring scale of piety whose gradations make collective unity an increasingly elusive possibility for Muslim feminists.

Nor is it a hidden divide; its ugly ramparts and the whizzing grenades each side lobs at the other are in plain view (perhaps problematically so) for those who may not have a stake in the debate. One recent moment when these came into view occurred around the commemoration of World Hijab Day, held annually on February 1.[2] This is an occasion where non-Muslim women could wear the veil to show solidarity with the many veiled and Muslim women. The website for World Hijab Day states "Better Awareness, Greater Understanding, Peaceful World" as its motto.[3] Offering stories of headscarf-wearing women, the general effort is to humanize these women, and hence end harassment that so many of them experience. When I last looked, there were no stories of women who choose to wear a full-face veil. The ones available feature Muslim women who have chosen to wear the hijab, their testimonies shaking up the stereotype that all women who veil are oppressed. Also provided are testimonials of non-Muslim women, participants in previous hijab days who gush over its many unexpected lessons ranging from an awareness of their own ignorance to a better understanding of Islam.

The assumption of World Hijab Day is of course that the headscarf and its stricter cousin the full-face veil are synonymous with Islam, required for its practice. Undoubtedly anti-headscarf proponents in places like France are complicit in this development—at least in contemporary terms, having forced a confrontation where an argument for not banning the headscarf relied for its strength on the false premise that it was in fact essential for Muslim practice. Preserving the *option* for some women who wished to wear the headscarf or the veil only resulted in entrenching its position as an incontrovertible prerogative of Muslim religious practice. This is not to say that conservative Muslims and Muslim eschatology in general have not promoted the picture of veiled woman as a true and best representative of the faith, routinely choosing women who wear the headscarf for public speaking events as visible spokespersons. At one time the Islamic Society of North America, the largest umbrella organization for American Muslims, required all female employees regardless of their faith to wear the headscarf on their premises.

The unveiled are expectedly perturbed by the construction of the truly pious Muslim woman as duly veiled; in the shadow of World Hijab Day 2016 Sara Yasin, a self-described hijab alum, wrote a post called "World Hijab Day has Got it All Wrong." In her piece Yasin takes issue both with the premise that the hijab protects women from the male gaze but also a series of pro-hijab cartoons that present a woman that is not wearing the hijab as an unwrapped lollipop or as rotting fruit. None of it, she rightly concludes, encourages an environment where the choice of wearing or not wearing a veil can be safely availed by women and recognized as a human right.

Unveiled and Muslim

In my own experience the issue of the veil, its wearing and non-wearing, is a festering and still-bleeding gash in the body of Muslim women as a collective. While many veiled and unveiled Muslim women including myself have pointed to their frustration with the West's preoccupation with the veil, the fact remains that until it exists not simply as an object but as a moral delineator. As such, it will continue to preclude the organization of Muslim women as a collective that can take on male dominance within the faith. The political cost wearing the veil in Western countries, where it increasingly exposes the wearers to harassment and religious profiling, forces the equation that these women— brave enough to declare a much maligned religious identity in public—are willing to take on the cost of being Muslim in a way that unveiled women are not. The sorts of appropriations that Muslim women have made of the "veil = pure" equation in Muslim countries are not really available in Western nations where the veil signifies something sinister and marginal and, if only partially, anonymous.

In the summer of 2009 I visited Egypt. I went as part of a delegation made up mostly of South Asian Muslims (some of whom lived in the United States) and American academics. This was still Mubarak's Egypt; the Arab Spring had not yet dawned nor been quashed by the military with its consequent bloodletting. In his speech, President Obama had sought "a new beginning between the United States and the Muslims of the world, one based on mutual interest and mutual respect." No one could have known what was coming then, but the divisions were still obvious. The academics and students that we met from the American University in Cairo were fluent in English and Westernized. Most were dressed in Western clothes and indeed seemed eager to underscore, particularly to the white Americans among our group, just how cosmopolitan and West-friendly they were.

At Cairo University, the very venue where President Obama gave his speech, there was more skepticism—particularly toward me. I was the only woman who was Muslim and who was not wearing a headscarf. Two of the three faculty members that we met were similarly Muslim women and both were wearing their headscarves. They asked me several times if I was Muslim and several times I said yes. They did not respond but they also did not engage; they seemed to imply that if I was Muslim, I should be dressed like they were, should choose to wear my Islam visibly. It was as if our sense of common experience and history, our opposition of imperialism and hegemony, was now irrelevant—a sideshow to my lack of a veil. In choosing not to wear it, my allegiances were suspect; I had chosen a team and it was not their team. I had also refused to wear the headscarf when we briefly visited Al-Azhar University, the oldest and most highly revered center for Islamic learning in the world. There had, however, been no other women present and so no stated objections to my omission.

Unspoken censure changed to loudly articulated disagreement toward the end of the trip. On this occasion we went to a large center devoted to the propagation of Islamic studies, located outside Cairo in one of the suburbs then named after various dates important to the then rulers of Egypt. The building was funded by a Qatari foundation and scholar and was large and imposing, a white swan among the suburban dunes of Cairo. Inside, over fifty young people, all employees of the foundation, awaited us. The topic was not only a mutual exchange of ideas but also to learn more about what they were doing to proliferate a moderate and inclusive Islam via the internet.

Inside, the arrangement was an unusual one: we the guests were lined up on chairs along one wall, foreign specimens of whom all must have a good view. Our audience sat opposite us in a similar line, the principals from the place in the first row with assumedly less important others behind them. The idea was to have a discussion, with questions posed by either side and then discussed among the group. So we began with the usual silence that inaugurates such plans—the reticence to speak first a common habit. Then, after a bit, things got going and we had the usual back and forth about the differences in forms of government, what mosques are like in the United States and so on. Ten or fifteen minutes into it, we got to the heart of the matter. One among them asked: "Given that the veil (the headscarf at least) is required in Islam, how could I stand or give answers about Muslim women, even really consider myself a good Muslim?" Behind her, silhouettes of heads nodded in appreciation and agreement; unveiled women were not to be called Muslim. This was an important topic.

With flaming, feverish cheeks I responded that I did not think I had to wear a veil, a headscarf like some in the audience or a face veil like others. My own interpretation of my faith did not see the practice as necessary, I said. I found it much more crucial and pressing, for instance, to work for social justice. I was working as a lawyer representing Muslim victims of domestic violence, and that, I believed, was the core of living my faith. No one heard the second portion of my answer; at that point a chorus of voices rose—exclamations against my obviously uninformed and incorrect perspective regarding the veil. Many objectors were men, who duly addressed me as sister, before proceeding to disdain my views.

In this cacophony, one of the Muslim men in our delegation gave a command for order. Its very tone foretold the authoritative and conclusive summation he was going to deliver to pacify the crowd, mend the tears that the catty women in the congregation had just made in the otherwise pristine fabric of cross-cultural exchange. "We understand that the dominant view in Islamic scholarship is that women must be modest and that modesty is interpreted variously as the covering of the hair and the face." Having delivered the mollifying morsel, he continued "of course not all of us on this side agree with each other"—suggesting clearly that the immorality of my unveiled state must not be attached to him—"and of course you may disagree with some of the people on this side of the room"—me. "But of course, we have all come here in the spirit of exchange, to listen and understand the other."

I had already lost him; I spent the rest of the day in an inflamed fury. On the bus back to Cairo many in the group, including, much to my utter disappointment, a white female academic, lauded our great male peacemaker for his efforts. If my female questioner had insisted that I was not a Muslim, this man, who lived and worked with unveiled Muslim women in the West (and would never have challenged their choice), had grasped the opportunity to do something in this climate more amenable to his perspective. Moral disciplining is done in a variety of ways, and that evening as I lay awake, replaying the morning in my mind with shame and anger and disappointment, I knew that this was one of them.

Veiled contexts

As an unveiled woman, there is a danger in recounting incidents such as these. The current construction of the veil both within Islam and beyond it is interested primarily and perhaps singularly in a yes-and-no vote, one that is reflected in whether the veil as object forms a part of one's daily attire. If this book, or chapter or paragraph or sentence is in any way a no, it is also a refusal of this very formulation. The raw recounting of these incidents, repeated numerous times in various other contexts, the times I have capitulated and veiled myself for the sake of belonging, for the sake of delivering some more important message in mosques or Islamic Centers that would not admit me otherwise, is presented for one purpose. That purpose is not to reveal or explicate the doctrinal truth or falsity of the veil, its necessity or optionality, not even its connection to context or history—but rather the emotional rancor, the unsoothed rawness with which it rends women, particularly Muslim women, apart.

The fissure created by the veil, by the moral scale attached to its avowal and disavowal, is the core obstacle that confronts Muslim feminism, while scholars like Fatima Mernissi and more recently Saher Amer have discussed at length the male-centric interpretations of religious doctrine that have led to the elevation of veiling as a requirement. There is, however, still a need to explore the consequences the disagreement over the veil has had to the relationships between Muslim women—and the extent to which this disagreement has permitted and promoted male interlopers, such as the man in Cairo, to intercede and impose their pronouncement. The questions then are not simply whether or not the veil is required, mandated, an essential tenet, but also what it accomplishes in the path of realizing a religious community that is not dictated by one or another interpretation, but rather inculcating respecting and maintaining a unity that has been elusive.

In a world framed in the crude language of "us and them," the veil has been marked and graded, and then attached to a constant and unforgiving moral judgment that is deemed to be a woman's unshakable burden. What is judged *by means* of an object is also reduced *to* an object and so it is with the veil. When there is no need to inquire further, to question or know, to go beyond the physical, the easily avowed and the visibly apprehended, the two entities, object and wearer, become synonymous, losing the possibility of subjectivity and becoming together one object. This single object is then judged permissible or impermissible and is always the signifier of one or another truth: either the rightness of Western opposition to the veil, or the correctness of the Islamist insistence on it.

3 REBELLION

When school was out the gates that were closed all day would be partially opened. I was picked up from a side gate outside which all males had to wait. Every now and then a younger brother would be given special permission to enter. Right in front of the gate were the raised platform and columns of what had probably been intended as an entrance to the school when it had been built in 1905. Now all the girls jostled for space on this platform whose height allowed us to see over the half-open gate and spot the brothers or fathers who had come to pick us up. Most of my friends left from the front gate.

There was however, one girl who waited here. During school, she was just like us, wore the uniform just like us, her long black braid also just like ours, hanging down her back. In the afternoon, when school let out, she leaned against the column just like us. When it was time to leave, she changed. In the space of a small second she removed a full veil from a pocket in her backpack. She put it on and disappeared inside. Then, she walked out of the gate and into the city.

The Finsbury Park Mosque is a four-story building that stands across from the Finsbury Park subway station in North

London. It is in a "diverse" area, a term that has over the years become code for areas that have significant population of immigrants and their descendants. That is exactly the implied meaning of the term when used in relation to this particular mosque. Frequented by Muslim immigrants from Pakistan, Somalia, and various parts of the Arab world, the mosque was inaugurated in 1994 by none other than Prince Charles himself. Those of course were somewhat different days for British Muslims. In the years after September 11 it has been raided several times and accused of harboring terrorists and weapons. In recent years, however, and under new leadership, the mosque has tried to update and clean up its image as a greenhouse for extremist ideology, holding open houses and welcoming non-Muslim community members inside, even putting women at the forefront of these events to emphasize their participation in mosque affairs.

Women who wear a full-face veil, or *niqab*, are common in this mosque—not a majority, but present in significant enough numbers so as to be a common sight in ways that they would not be in most places. It is here on an evening in June 2012 that Rebekah Dawson and her brother had an altercation with a volunteer caretaker of the mosque. Its reasons stemmed from a simmering and often boiling-over conflict that had riven the mosque leadership for some time. One faction, the one to which Dawson, her brother, and husband belonged, did not believe that it was permissible to allow non-Muslim Westerners to be taken on tours around the mosque. The caretaker in question had recently taken a group of Portuguese visitors who were not appropriately dressed (with heads, arms, and legs covered) for a tour of the mosque. This last incident prompted Dawson's husband to go to the mosque and beat up the caretaker volunteer. For this act, Dawson's husband was duly arrested and charged with assault.

Shortly after the arrest of her husband, Rebekah Dawson, fully veiled and accompanied by her brother, arrived at the Finsbury Park Mosque in search of the caretaker. According to his court testimony, Dawson found the man and then, while still wearing her niqab, threatened him with dire consequences if he chose to testify against her husband in the assault case.[1] The volunteer caretaker, supported by the remainder of the faction that wanted a more open mosque, complained again to the police. Dawson, still wearing the full-face veil, was arrested. She was charged with one count of intimidation of a potential witness.

Britain in 2012 was already a country long up in arms over the cultural devastation that many on country's political far right associated with multiculturalism, which required the toleration of idiosyncratic (in their view) and oppressive (also in their view) religious practices such as the full-face veil. When Dawson's case came up for hearing at the Blackfriars Crown Court, the stage was set for a joust—it is exactly what followed. Dawson, the defendant, refused to remove her niqab. The only means by which her identity could be affirmed was when she went into a separate room with a female arresting officer and removed her veil.

The Crown Court judge did not feel that a proper trial could proceed with the defendant wearing a full-face veil—her features, expression, and demeanor invisible to the jury and judge charged with determining her guilt or innocence. On August 13, 2012, he asked the defendant to remove her veil. She refused to do so. Following this event he ordered a stay in the trial itself for consideration of the issue of whether a defendant, in this case Rebekah Dawson, could be compelled to remove her face veil while being tried for intimidation in a criminal trial. He also commissioned an expert report on the issue of whether a full-face veil is required, as the defendant claimed, as part of Islamic religious practice.

The thirty-six-page decision Judge Peter Murphy issued on the matter is a hefty document that does a better job of cataloging the UK's confusion over multiculturalism and what counts as "tolerance" of other religions and their varying and often confounding precepts, than a consideration of whether masking one's face is any real hurdle in the ability of a jury (or anyone else) to gauge the truth or falsity of a person's representation. In the decision Judge Murphy opines on an expansive variety of subjects. He dismisses the expert's "stark" conclusion, which holds that Dawson has a right to wear the niqab in court. Following this dismissal is a meandering extra-judicial consideration of everything: from the fact that not all Muslim women choose to wear a face veil, a fact he says can be witnessed by simply walking down the street, to various excerpts from the Muslim Council of

Britain, to consideration of Islamic religious edicts regarding the wearing of the full-face veil.

In the end, he uses the law to justify his decision, which he insists is required to create a uniform precedent on how the issue must be dealt with in courts all over Britain. Dawson, he rules, can wear the full-face veil in court, but not while she is presenting evidence (i.e., testifying as a witness). The import of his decision is simple: a judge in a courtroom can order a woman wearing a full-face veil to remove it when she takes the stand. In the case before him, Dawson had to remove the face veil while she testified. She was convicted of intimidation and issued a twenty-month sentence in prison.

The pivotal irony of Dawson's case—that she, a woman wearing a full-face veil, had attempted to intimidate a man—is not discussed in the decision. It is a pity because it is that crucial aspect—the power and possibility presented by the deliberate anonymity and intentional subterfuge that the veil represents—that was the real ghost in the Blackfriar's courtroom. The idea that a completely veiled woman, in having recalibrated the balance in person-to-person interactions, equals, even in the sole sense of being fully masked, a threat was not something that was considered.

Yet it is this purported aspect of the full-face veil to appear threatening, to meddle with the calculations of who we are as who we are seen to be, that perhaps dictated Judge Murphy's ruling. Those who do not operate within the court system of a Western nation may not understand the careful choreography that is the criminal trial. Elaborate rules govern everything from where the people sit to when one stands to who gets to speak and when and what gets to be said. Within this carefully ordered environment, in which each utterance and all movements take place per sets of rules (Judge Murphy does at one point in his decision quote the Bench book), the appearance of a fully veiled woman whose countenance is hidden from plain view is herself an aberration, a flouting of the ordered predictability of the courtroom.

There is power not simply in procedure and who gets to dictate it, but also in the optics that go with it. The hiding of one's face, particularly in a venue where one's identity is key, rebels against that very premise of order and control. There are rules to be upheld here and the primacy and sovereignty of the judge and the law must impose and uphold a visible order. In this sense, Dawson's actions suggest the issue of breaking two rules: the one that she is formally accused of violating and the one protecting the decorum of the courtroom that assumes that all will present their faces, their identities, openly and visibly.

Interestingly, one of the cases that Judge Murphy discusses in his voluble decision involves not a defendant but rather a prosecution witness. In Ottawa, Canada, a few years before Rebekah Dawson went to the Finsbury Mosque to threaten her husband's accuser, a woman spoken of only as "NS" was a witness in a trial for sexual abuse against her father and brother.[2] In that case, NS refused to testify in court without her full-face veil and the case progressed all the way to the Canadian Supreme Court.

If intentions are important, then the ones of the veiled woman in Canada were markedly different from those of Rebekah Dawson. She is identified as NS to protect her identity as a survivor of sexual abuse. While she wore the full-face veil outside court as well, she wished *particularly* to wear it inside the courtroom because it provided a level of insulation, a mask so to speak, that would save her from the trauma of meeting the gaze of her alleged abusers.

The issue, however, was not so simple. The Canadian trial judge had to evaluate whether NS's belief in wearing the veil was "sincere." In the United States, judges are precluded from evaluating the sincerity of a person's religious beliefs because of the constitutional separation between church and state. Such requirements do not encumber judges in the UK and apparently in Canada. The trial judge found that she was not sincere enough in her choice to wear the full-face veil because she had removed it when the picture for her driver's license was taken. This was a strike against her, an indication that she was posturing. This issue of sincerity becomes even more important because it is the basis on which the judge makes the ultimate decision as to whether the advantages of forcing a woman to unveil outweigh the advantages of allowing her to wear the veil. The Supreme Court found that the simple evidence that NS had taken her veil off for her driver's license picture was not enough to prove "insincerity" of belief and that the trial court should reconsider that portion of its decision.

It hit hard, however, on the other basis of deciding whether NS must be forced to remove the veil. One of the rights cited in favor of requiring her to do so was the defendant's right to a fair trial. To insure a fair trial, the court noted, the judge and jury are entitled to evaluate the credibility of a witness. If she were to keep her full-face veil on, the effectiveness of cross-examination could be affected by the fact that her face was not visible. Secondly, the court also concluded that the jury could not properly assess NS's credibility if her face was covered. For all these crisply articulated reasons, the Canadian court found that "NS," an alleged victim of sexual abuse, would be required to remove her face veil when she testified. When the case was remanded back to the trial court, NS refused to testify and the charges against the men were dismissed.

Truth, then, at least in the view of most courts, is presumed to reside in our faces, in the equality of exchange that is assumed when one person looks at another. Full-face veils, in being objects whose primary purpose is to obscure most of the face, are barriers to truth. There are, however, problems with this assumption. The case of NS is an iteration of just how flimsy the assumption is. As a member of a minority religious and ethnic community in Canada, NS undoubtedly faced huge challenges in speaking out about the sexual abuse she faced at the hands of family members. Nevertheless, she chose to do so, and even while the courts tried to tread middle ground on the issue—by holding that she could choose to continue wearing the veil while in the courtroom but not while testifying—their decision may well stop others in her position from coming forward with similar complaints, knowing that they would have to reveal their faces.

The hiding of one's face as a means of avoiding censorious gazes, or doing so only in moments where one finds it to be threatening, is not unusual in Muslim countries. As a child, I routinely saw my grandmother, who normally only covered her head, taking the edge of her large scarf in her mouth and holding it as a means of obscuring most of her face. This happened only when we found ourselves in crowds composed mostly of men, in the middle of crowded bazaars or at a shop in which a group of men had suddenly entered. This action can also be seen in Pakistan when women are involved in court proceedings. Before cameras from the media, these women who normally only cover their heads will take on the full-face veil in an effort to hide their identities from publication. In some cases, they will even give interviews only while their faces are obscured.

There are many reasons for this practice, notably and expectedly the fact that women thrust into the public eye by crime and circumstance cannot be blamed for wanting to obscure their identity and prevent its publication. Exposure in the public sphere, even if it is only due to the misfortune of being a victim of crime, can bring the wrong sorts of attention, incurring costs that could ruin reputations and bring shame to families. The face veil as an object presents a way out of this for women who may not be used to public lives, frequenting courtrooms and giving statements before television cameras, or even simply being in bazaars, where men dominate; it presents a way of being, but not necessarily interacting, with the space and its challenges.

The two cases above present an interesting contrast. In one, Rebekah Dawson is able to threaten and intimidate a man working at the Finsbury Park Mosque, even while she is wearing a full-face veil. It is necessary to wonder how instrumental the veil was in her ability to deliver a death threat to a man. Did she believe that her anonymity in this instance would provide her with a cover against future charges? In an odd sort of way, did the veil, in its conferral of anonymity, enable her to feel more powerful, even in a negative and threatening way? Given that the entire struggle at the Finsbury Park Mosque was one that took place between mostly conservative factions, her belonging to the one would normally have precluded her from seeking out conversations with anonymous men. The veil, however, seems to have enabled her to overcome that objection, permitting her, in her own eyes at least, to take on a strange man and even to threaten him.

The case of NS presents the other side of the veil but points again to how some women who wear it may consider it a means of equalizing an exchange in a male-dominated public sphere, using it as a buffer, a form of control over themselves that resists the male gaze. Nowhere does this become more important than when males in question have sexually assaulted women. [Testimony and research reveals that women of all backgrounds often dread confronting their accusers in a courtroom setting, let alone testifying against them.] In the case of NS, the veil functioned as a means of avoiding that confrontation, that inherent intimidation that could not only re-traumatize NS but also affect her ability to testify fully. Invisibility can be a means of altering the power dynamic of a particular environment in a way that cedes control to women who may not otherwise have it.

There is also the thorny matter of the truth and its connection to our faces and their expressions. It is not only Canadian courts in the matter of NS that have insisted that the demeanor of a witness is crucial and must be visible for a jury to determine the truth; courts in most Western countries have made similar determinations. In the United States, this precedent relies on the premise that any defendant has the right to confront their accuser. All of this, however, has recently been proven untrue.

Several years after the Canadian Supreme Court made its decision, a researcher named Amy May-Leach at the University of Ontario Institute of Technology began her own investigation.[3] Leach designed a study whose purpose was to have subjects guess the truthfulness of women with and without veils. Published in the *Journal of the American Psychiatric Association*, Leach's study used female volunteers who were asked to wear their normal attire and shown one of two videos: one showed a person keeping close watch on a backpack; the other showed a person rifling through the backpack. After they had seen the videos, the women were then taken to another room to be questioned by a mock prosecution and defense. Regardless of which video they had seen, the women were instructed to insist throughout the questioning that they had not witnessed a theft.

Recordings of the questionings were then shown to a second set of volunteers who were asked to guess whether the women had told the truth. For unveiled women, the volunteers guessed correctly at a rate of about 50 percent, the same rate as if they had flipped a coin. It was only when the women were veiled (by headscarf or the full-face veil) that the guessing rate improved significantly beyond chance percentages. Leach conducted this first level of the study in Canada, then repeated the study in the UK and the Netherlands, and found similar results in both cases.

Leach, who worked as a border security agent prior to becoming a researcher, said that the results of the study were surprising to many who believed that assessing a person's facial expressions is crucial to discerning whether they are being truth or deceptive. Her own experience as a border security agent led her to believe otherwise, a suspicious that was proven by her study. Instead of being distracted by facial cues like smiles or raised eyebrows, which are often incorrect, the volunteers who watched recordings of veiled women concentrated on the facts and substance of what the women were saying—which in general are better indicators of whether someone is telling the truth.

Veils on trial

In the summer of 2016, a complete ban on full-face veils came into effect in Switzerland.[4] The issue of the veil and its permissibility had been brewing for several years. In 2013, the Swiss voted in huge numbers (65 percent) in favor of a complete ban. The statute that eventually resulted from the referendum imposes a huge fine of 9,200 Euros on any woman who is found wearing a full-face veil. To facilitate the enforcement of the law, the Swiss government printed brochures in Arabic to be distributed in areas of the country where there were significant Arab and Muslim populations. Classes were also designed to teach police officers how to deal with women who were breaking the law. These lessons would be put to use. In the Swiss canton of Ticino, which had been the first to introduce the ban, citizens were eager for it to be enforced. On July 7, 2016, two activists, one a Muslim convert and another a French-Algerian businessman, were fined for having been found wearing the burka as part of protests in that town.

The arguments, in Switzerland and in other places that have banned the burka, are varied—ranging from security issues, to the right to see other people who are inhabiting the public sphere, to the argument that the burka is not religiously required in Islam. One lesser-known argument is the Swiss aversion to the aesthetic transformation of their public sphere by the wearing of such a garment. This dimension becomes more apparent when one considers Switzerland's burka ban in connection with another ban that came into effect a few years earlier.

On November 29, 2009, a nationwide referendum was held on minarets, the tall column-like buildings that often (but not always) are a fixture of Islamic mosques. The ban passed, an overwhelming majority voting in favor of prohibiting any future construction of minarets in Switzerland. Many found the results surprising; while the Danish cartoon controversy had recently rocked Europe, analysts had predicted that the ban would fail. Furthermore, minarets were not a common fixture in the country, neither numerous nor visible.

According to scholar Todd Green, who wrote about the issue in the journal *Church and State* in 2010, there were at the time only four minarets in Switzerland.[5] Located in Geneva, Zurich, and two smaller cities, the minarets had not been the subject of controversy or attention. A ban on them seemingly also went again the commitment to religious freedom that was a crucial facet of both Swiss and EU law. Nor could the Swiss ban be argued away as an issue of a religious symbol in a public space deemed to be secular. The aesthetic landscape of Switzerland is littered with many iterations of faith, cathedrals, and churches, their steeples rising into the horizon in every Swiss town. The real issue, as Green points out, is one of aesthetic control of which and whose religious symbols occupy the public space and are hence considered permissible.

Considering the burka ban in conjunction with the minaret ban permits us to understand how long-standing ideas of what public space should look like cohere with other forces. Islamophobia, anti-immigrant views, and a general fear of losing a certain nativist concept of public space cohere and find voice in a ban on the burka. The battle, then, is as much on the issue of aesthetics and their transformation as it is on the issue of women's rights or security concerns, or the belief that people have the right to see whom they are engaging with. The insistence on wearing the burka is in this sense a subversion of precisely this premise, making a minority who sees its visibility being treated as a threat, using the deliberately assumed invisibility of the burka as a form of protest.

An analysis of burka bans in Europe, which are now in place in France, the Netherlands, Belgium, Bulgaria, and Switzerland among others—under the rubric of use of visibility and invisibility as a form of protest or subversion of a mainstream aesthetic ideal that excludes the minority "other"—is a useful one. Such an analysis refuses to locate the discussion (as it often has been) in a decontextualized and depoliticized theology, in ideas of whether or not it is required by Islam. By focusing instead on the interplay between the politics of the context and the use of the symbol in the public sphere, we can reveal dimensions in which the state and largely white majorities of various European countries are trying to control the aesthetics of the public sphere. These aesthetics are selected not simply because of their religious character, or because they are connected to Islam; they are made because they provoke among the white Western public the very sentiments of exclusion, intolerance, and inflexibility that they wish to expose. There is a difference, however, when directed toward the veil: all of these sentiments are legitimate and justified, the backbone of other disparagements and new instruments of marginalization. Invisibility is put into the service of making visible something otherwise intangible; the burka in the European context becomes an instrument of exposure, in opposition to its physical, literal, and aesthetic capacities.

Beyond Europe, the interplay between veil, visibility, and public space changes yet again. The same summer in which the Swiss veil ban came into effect, a similar ban was being considered in, of all places, Egypt. It is notable that the ban being considered would not (as in the case of France) apply to the Islamic headscarf or even the niqab, in which a woman covers half her face but leaves her eyes visible. The burka, as interpreted by the proposed law, is a garment that covers a woman from head to toe and leaves only a mesh in front of her face. This burka is most commonly used in Afghanistan, Pakistan, and Saudi Arabia.

When legislators in the Egyptian Parliament debated the proposed bill, they took refuge in religion. Amna Nossier, one of the members of Parliament who backed the bill and who is also a professor of comparative jurisprudence at Cairo's Al-Azhar University,[6] argued not only that this kind of veil (as opposed to the headscarf) was not required by Islamic tradition, but also that it had been worn by Jews at the time of the Holy Prophet. The statement is an important one, not least in its effort to dislocate the burka from Islamic practice, but also in that it goes further and locates its inauthenticity by connecting it to Jewish practice.

The expurgation of pre-Islamic practices that have seeped into Islam, and whose extrication is necessary for the reclamation of "pure" Islam, is a project that is dear to Muslim revivalists. Locating a ban on the burka within this Islamic reclamation is a clever and different strategy, although whether it will work is unclear. Months have passed since the introduction of the bill and as of January 2017, it had not yet passed. At the same time, various restrictions on wearing the niqab (a different form of face covering which leaves the eyes visible) have already been instated in several state-affiliated public institutions. Doctors, nurses, and various faculty members at Cairo University, for instance, are not permitted to wear even the niqab.

Another Muslim country, however—not far from Egypt—did go ahead with a burka ban. In the first week of 2017, officials from the Ministry of Interior in Morocco took to the major markets in the country.[7] They went into shops and stalls that sold women's garments and distributed a letter; its contents read simply, "We have observed that you are engaged in the sale or manufacture of full face veils." Like the Egyptians, the Moroccan document argued that a veil of this sort was not required in Islam and that the merchants must "stop the manufacture and sale of the burka" immediately or face action by the government.

The Moroccan and Egyptian overtures against the niqab are anomalies in an obvious sense. There are, of course, several Muslim countries, most notably Saudi Arabia and Iran, which *require* women to cover their hair. Similarly, Turkey, until the recent ascent of center-right and Islamist-affiliated Erdoğan, banned all forms of the veil, including the headscarf. Using state power to abridge or enforce or control women's clothing is not something new in these Muslim nations. At the same time, the trend in Egypt and Morocco, the interest in distinguishing between different kinds of veils, does represent a new direction. Its impetus seems to lie in using state power to influence the construction and interpretation of different *kinds* of veiling practices. Knowing that these novel forms of the veil are championed by various extremist groups, their de-legitimization is seen as crucial, a taking back of state power to toe the line between the extreme interpretation that a burka is seen to represent and the moderate interpretation that a headscarf is the required alternative.

Just as the interplay of politics and symbolism defines the significance of the veil in places like Switzerland and France, so it is in Morocco and Egypt. It is worth mentioning, therefore, that Morocco, a constitutional monarchy, is using monarchical fiat to push through a ban that may otherwise have met with opposition (particularly among Islamists) had it undergone debate and been parsed via the bicameral requirements of most democracies. Similarly, Egypt's current political iteration involves a military ruler who overthrew an elected prime minister in a coup. That prime minister hailed from Egypt's Islamist party, whose followers would likely not have approved of any abridgment of the blanket permissibility of any kinds of veils.

A veil's aesthetics, the interplay of literal visibility and invisibility, are catalyzed by its context to reveal rebellion against the xenophobia of the French or Swiss. In these countries, electoral majorities coalesce around a collective suspicion of Muslims, and referenda are used to push through veil bans (and in some cases headscarf and minaret bans). Within Arab Muslim countries like Egypt and Morocco, the absence of a robust democracy and supportive majorities that would be anti-burka permits governments that are either held up by monarchies or have taken power in military coups to introduce a ban on the burka, a particular kind of veil, as a moderate middle ground. Finally, it must be noted that the state imprimatur given to these bans creates, as is nearly always the case, an incentive for those who wish to position themselves as rebels to avow the burka—the full-face veil—as a symbol of their rebellion.

These complications of context prove one of the most crucial, and most ignored, truths about the veil: independent of context, it does not have much meaning.

4 FEMINISM

In late 2010 I traveled to Boston to talk about drones. The talk I was supposed to give focused on what it was like to be on the other side, to be watched, and always worried that some pattern of activity would lead the faraway operator to fire. During the day, I rode the train with two other graduate students who were attending the conference. We knew each other but only barely, so our conversation orbited the general topic of the conference: human rights, surveillance, and just war. Male graduate students have fervent opinions on these issues and they were no different.

On the train, two of us sat, one of us stood. The train stopped and a woman entered the otherwise empty car. She wore a long and loose black abaya that covered her from head to toe. Her face was also covered, except the small space between her forehead and her nose that allowed her to see. She wore glasses. Our conversation stopped completely. She stared straight ahead except for a single moment when our eyes met. The train stopped again, we all stepped out.

We stayed silent; she passed us and ascended the escalator. We lingered behind, the other two getting on before me. They *looked up at the woman who was almost at the top and then at each other. They started laughing. I could not laugh, but I smiled.*

In 1996 a young Pakistani artist named Shahzia Sikander screened a performance-art piece in Chicago.[1] It featured Sikander wearing an elaborate lace veil for several weeks. The reactions of her various friends and peers were recorded and then exhibited as part of a digital installation. In an interview about her experience developing the piece, Sikander said, "It was wonderful to not have people see my facial or body language, and at the same time be in control and know that they did not know I was acting, and checking their reaction."

Five years later, a little over a month after the terrorist attacks on the Twin Towers and the Pentagon, there was another public spectacle featuring a full-face veil. On October 14, 2001, Democratic congresswoman Caroline Maloney of New York donned a full burka[2] on the floor of the House of Representatives. Passionately arguing for an attack on Afghanistan, Maloney presented a sensationalist account of what it was like to wear the full-face veil. "It's hard to breathe," Maloney reported. "It's particularly hard to see, there's a mesh in front of the eyes and it's like having 15 screen doors in front of you, it's very demeaning, it's as if you have no identity." For all of these reasons, Maloney argued bombing Afghanistan was the "just war" that Americans "had to wage."

Between the representation by a Muslim feminist artist and an American woman arguing for war, the latter won out. What Maloney said was echoed again and again by American feminists who saw war as necessary to "free" Afghan women from the oppressive burkas that were imprisoning them. Her argument was echoed by First Lady Laura Bush[3] when she called on all members of the civilized world to support bombing Afghanistan, the war's visual being freeing Afghan women from the burka. In support of the project, many White House officials wore little snips of blue cloth on their lapels, the burka and the bombing thus intermixed in the American imagination.

Heads of feminist organizations ecstatically joined the call for a feminist war on the burka. A few months after Maloney's speech, a coalition of Western women's organizations sent a direct letter to then president George Bush,[4] asking him "to take emergency action to save the lives and secure the future of Afghan women." Its signatories included Eleanor Smeal, president of the Feminist Majority Foundation in Virginia, together with other notable feminists such as Gloria Steinem, Eve Ensler, Meryl Streep, and Susan Sarandon. Women in the United States overwhelmingly support the war, they noted, because it will "liberate Afghan women from abuse and oppression."

Nor was this letter the end of it. The Feminist Majority Foundation, one of the biggest feminist organizations in the United States, developed a campaign titled "Stop Gender Apartheid in Afghanistan."[5] As feminist scholars have pointed out, the Feminist Majority's campaign assumed that Afghan women had to be taught to liberate themselves and that white feminists would do the teaching, even as the

United States dropped bombs on the country. The campaign's inordinate focus on the veil as a central symbol reflected this very orientalist perspective, where an alteration in the clothes these women wore was central to the project of delivering empowerment to them. In its own communications, the Feminist Majority was quick and eager to congratulate itself on the success of its campaign in language that was rather similar to the language of the Bush administration, reiterating the "draconian" measures imposed by the Taliban and by reporting "successes" as women being seen in the street without burkas.

The Feminist Majority's example was aped by other organizations. Not long after the invasion of Afghanistan, Amnesty International issued a poster aimed at mobilizing action around CEDAW, the Convention of Elimination of Discrimination Against Women. The poster featured a shot of a crowd of women all in blue burkas. The camera looks down at these women. Only one has her face uncovered. A ray of light shines on her face as she looks up. The message of the poster is the same as Maloney's assertion: a single garment is the core of the repression faced by Afghan women.

American female journalists venturing into Afghanistan to expose the repressive conditions of Afghan women's lives were also obsessed with the veil. The *New York Times* Afghan correspondent Alissa Rubin, in the *New York Times Magazine* on May 5, 2011,[6] wrote: "I felt rejected with my burqa down, like I was not good enough to be seen in public. I leaned in the back seat and felt a wash of passivity come over me. Nothing was demanded of me except silence." The real silencing, of course, was that of real Afghan women. As early as 2001, the Revolutionary Association of Afghan Women issued a statement[7] that said that an end of the mandatory burka was in no way "an indication of women's rights and liberties in Afghanistan." In their eagerness to *see* Afghan women, these white female saviors, who made the veil central to their campaign, forgot to *listen* to them.

*

The veiled and the exotic

The equation of the veil as the aesthetic of the exotic—and hence submissive—"other" did not emerge with the US war in Afghanistan, of course. Its historic precursor was the colonial harem, whose iterations of female seclusion and subjugation first married feminism with imperialism. The origin of the aesthetic of the veil as a simultaneous realm which the colonial project sought to conquer and an emblem of the repressive reality of colonized peoples emerged in the early years of the colonial period. In 1981, an Algerian writer and historian living in France, Malek Alloula, published a book of reproduced postcards sent back by French soldiers in Algeria in the first three decades of the 1800s. Nearly all the photographs featured veiled women. In his essays, published alongside the photographs, Alloula pointed out how many of the women featured in them were forced to unveil so that their pictures could be taken. The camera had only recently been invented.[8]

The second essay in Alloula's book is titled "Women from the Outside: Obstacle and Transparency" and features eight photographs of women, all but one of whom are wearing full-face veils. The first and third photographs are both titled "Moorish Women Taking a Walk" and the second "Moorish women on their way to the cemetery." Nearly all the women in all the pictures are dressed in white. In the first photograph, which features the smallest group of women, one on the immediate right holds the hand of a small child. The last woman in the same picture seems older, bent forward and walking with a cane. In the second photograph, featuring women bound for the cemetery, two little girls, their faces uncovered, pause before the table of a man who seems to be selling something. The third photograph features the largest number of women, most of them crossing a bridge. Some again are holding the hands of children, a few men walk before them.

These first photographs are important ones, for they are the only ones in the book that feature the women as they would have appeared in these public spaces even if they were not being photographed. "The first thing the foreign eye catches about Algerian women is that they are concealed from sight," writes Alloula at the beginning of the essay. The veiled Algerian women in the photographs, he notes, impose a kind of impotence: "the opaque veil that covers her intimates clearly and simply a refusal." A message is conveyed to the photographer that rejects the overture of taking a picture, discouraging the voyeurism of the photographer and immediately inflicting boundaries. It is, Alloula notes, a "triple rejection": a rejection of desire, a rejection of his "art" of photography and finally a rejection of place. The last underscores that while he may be present, the photographer does not belong, is an intruder. The whiteness of the veil— all the veils in this chapter are white—is a "symbolic equivalent of blindness."

That the colonial gaze could be so interested in capturing an image and yet be blind to what it seeks to capture is a great summation of the colonial project as a whole. Alloula notes the aptitude of this metaphor: whiteness is the absence of an image, of individuality and noted identity. The women, all swathed in white, imply a sameness, purposefully assuming the very reductionism that colonialism imposes when it seeks conquest: natives indistinguishable, lacking in complexity or variety. The white veils worn by the Algerian women are masks, barriers that resist penetration. The photographs that capture them outside, in public spaces, featured in this chapter always show more than one woman. Because the veils are identical, so are the images of the women. While it is not intentional, the photographer capturing them is cornered into a duplication of image, a repetition, an avowal of a group instead of an individual. Veils thus are a form of resistance and rebellion, an extension of the private space of the harem where they are protected, into the public realm where they may encounter a Western photographer.

The last three photographs in the chapter are different. Taken indoors or within private spaces, they feature single women and their gradual unveiling. The first of the three shows a white veiled woman, her veil obscuring all but her eyes. In the second picture, another veiled woman lifts up her arms; her face and hands remain unseen. The final picture in the chapter is also of a single Algerian woman; her face and part of her breast are uncovered. She squints at the camera, her arm raised up and above her head. She is indoors, standing before a woven tapestry. She is now exposed.

The vast majority of the remaining photographs in Alloula's book—and there are many of them—feature unveiled women. As he documents, some of these women were forced to unveil and posed so that French photographers or soldiers could take pictures of them. In other cases, they were models, "recruited from the margins of society" and posed so that they would appear to be the real thing. Curated by Alloula, the photographs are presented as a succession, beginning with the veiled woman, to the posed woman, and finally photographs of harems, those private female spaces that represent in a very literal sense the penetration of the forbidden, the previously sealed off.

As these photographs were meant for reproduction as postcards, the act of penetrating the harem came full circle, a vicarious conquest to be experienced not simply by the occupying forces that accomplished the dissolution of barriers but also by those at home. These photographs are not the work of a surreptitious and sneaky voyeur trying to get a few pictures of a realm that has been forbidden to him. These photographs feature Algerian woman unveiled and engaged in a variety of rituals, pouring tea or smoking water pipes. The inclusion of the activity is important because it highlights that the witnessing is not incidental, that the photographer has become part of the activity of this formerly forbidden and veiled space.

The initial recipients of these postcards may not have noticed the resignation on the faces of some of these women, nor been bothered by the disconnect between their expressions and conditions. Here are half-clothed women who had to pose before a stranger, a foreign man who was capturing their images. In order for their desirability as the "odalisque" to be communicated to the Western viewer, their sexuality had to be expressed boldly, unmistakably; being unveiled and visible is not enough. Instead, as Alloula notes, "One odalisque is lying down with her blouse indecently wide open," and there are many others, their breasts exposed as they sit with other women, as they smoke a water pipe, pour tea.

All the photographs in the final chapter of Alloula's book feature women with exposed breasts. There is no eroticism here, but instead a kind of pornography that seems to subsist on the complete reversal of power that has occurred between the book's initial photographs, women refusing to be seen, women protected beneath the portable privacy of the veil, and women not yet penetrated by the gaze of the colonial photographer. That photographer has by now conquered completely: not only is the veil removed, poor women unveiled and posed, the harem entered, the activities recorded, but they are now sexually available to the photographer and to the viewer. The ruse of incidental presence, the deliberate arrangement, is now completely abandoned; the sexual submission of the model to the photographer who controls all, can see all, to constitute not some subtle eroticism but pornography, is complete.

The concluding photograph is a summation of the veil's aesthetic subsumed into the story of colonial conquest. One of the most famous images from Alloula's book is this last one. A woman wearing a full-face veil stares back into the camera. On her chest, the folds of the dark veil are parted to reveal her bare breasts; all other parts of her body are concealed. Here is ultimate conquest: the female colonial subject now re-veiled to be an object of titillation. The function of the veil is annihilated; it no longer functions as a barrier, a form of rebellion or resistance against incursion. It is now completely an object of control whose use is determined by the photographer, who can order his subject to put it on or take it off or use it to cover her face, even as he demands that it expose her breasts. As Alloula writes, "The harem has become a brothel," bawdy and procured with the sad faces of the wage-earning women representing the impotence of the conquered.

Inside the harem: From veiled faces to veiled spaces

Entering and conquering the harem remains a symbol of potency; photographs of women taking refuge within its veiled geographical space a recurring fantasy seems to inspire Westerners through the ages. While the photographs in Alloula's study spanned the three decades following the French campaign in Algeria in 1830, others came earlier on the heels of the initial invasion. This included among others the French painter Delacroix, who was sent to North Africa [in 1832] as part of a French diplomatic mission. Once there, Delacroix, likely facilitated by the locals' desire to make good with the new men in charge, was able to enter an actual harem. Inside, he was transfixed: "I am like a man in a dream, seeing things he fears will vanish from him."[9]

Delacroix would not let them vanish. Indeed, he knew exactly why he had been sent as part of the mission. His historical paintings were well known and the French king was quite concerned about establishing both cultural and political dominance in the Mediterranean. Delacroix delivered with aplomb, feverishly sketching the entire duration of the trip. *The Women of Algiers*, Delacroix's masterpiece, was displayed in the May Salon in 1834, the year when French military control of Algeria was established. Unlike earlier artists who had indulged French curiosity about the odalisques of the Orient, Delacroix had actually *been* inside the harem. This lent his painting an air of authenticity, of being scientific in its representations.

It was neither of these things. A comparison with Alloula's photographs reveals an arrangement not very different from some of the mid-period postcards where the harem, the womens' clothing, the predictable objects, rugs and water pipes, and the black slave all place it squarely within typical representations. As Alloula points out in his book,[10] admission into the harem transformed the veil from a physical object to a physical space and hence the transition was made from veiled faces to veiled spaces. Consequently, unveiling was not a removal of the veil but the entry into a space, and in the case of painters and photographers, representation of that space. None of the women in the Delacroix painting are veiled, but their very appearance is a mark of submission toward the painter, who has not only entered the space but is now representing it. It is their unveiling and the representation of the harem from the inside that represents colonial conquest. Those earlier viewers of *Femmes Algerienne* could share with the painter the witnessing of forbidden space and forbidden women, both of which were now visible and available.

Delacroix's painting endured, and still does almost 200 years later. The years after its initial exhibition saw the emergence of several copies, all of them whetted by the intense curiosity of a French public that could not get enough of the exotic Orient in its newly conquered reality. The most famous resurrection of the painting came over a century later, when Picasso, long obsessed with the painting, made no less than fifteen versions of it between 1954 and 1955. He began painting them in the same month as the war for independence began in Algeria. The paintings, one of which would later go on to fetch the largest price ever, featured the women of Delacroix's work. The sumptuous colors and furnishings remain, but the women themselves are abstracted, to the extent of appearing only remotely human. The attempt at reconstruction from bits and pieces of the past represented perhaps the reconstitution of a people following the intrusion and destruction wrought by colonialism.

Afghan girls, Afghan lovers, Western photographers

Western photographers and journalists remain obsessed with entering and capturing, either in photographs or in stories. The photographer Steven McCurry's rendition of the *National Geographic* cover featuring the "Afghan Girl"[11] is counted among the five most resonant images that the magazine has ever published. The story of how McCurry procured the photograph sounds familiar when juxtaposed against the enduring Western obsession of piercing the veil or the boundaries represented by it. McCurry took the picture at a refugee camp in Pakistan in 1985. He did not know her name, and while he insists that he asked her permission, his lack of fluency in Urdu or Pashto, the two languages she may have spoken, suggests that he quite likely did not.

The woman's name was Sharbat Gula, and in 2002, *National Geographic* and McCurry himself decided to "find" her. What had generated curiosity and revenues decades earlier would likely do so again. In the articles and interviews published about the quest, much is made of the fact that the Afghan girl in the picture, being pre-pubescent, was free to roam. Now grown, she would have retreated behind the full-face veil into anonymity—not a problem for the persistence of Western media, however. Following a great deal of expenditure, the development of time-lapse models of aging and other technology, and likely also in payments to local informers, she was finally found and made to pose for more pictures, her now middle-aged and less fetching reality presenting to *National Geographic* readers the same thesis: of the backward, crude reality of the Afghan native. McCurry and *National Geographic* probably made a good bundle from the 2002 resurrection of the "Afghan Girl." Sharbat Gula herself was arrested in 2016 in Pakistan; she did not have the money to afford her bus fare.

An even more literal (and recent) conquest of the seclusion of the Afghan harem is described in *New York Times* journalist Rod Nordland's *The Lovers*,[12] which tells the tale of a pair of young star-crossed lovers whose story Nordland first reported in 2014 in *New York Times*. In this particular instance, Nordland and his team, a photographer and a videographer, are hot on the trail of a couple [where?] that has run off and hidden because they have married against the wishes of most of their families. Nordland compulsively calls them and their various relatives, to no avail. Undeterred by the fact that they may not want to be found, Nordland persists. He learns that the boy's father, who is not opposed to the match, knows where they are hiding. He cuts a deal with the man, promising to pay his transportation costs if he will lead them to the couple. The man, desperately poor, agrees and the caravan of *Times* employees makes its way to the remote village where Zakia and Ali are hiding.

When they reach their destination, they find that Ali is not present. His wife, the young Zakia, retreats to the women's quarters. The *Times* photographer, however, has waited too long and will not be deterred. He "pretends" not to know that he is not permitted into the women's spaces of the house, breaks in, and takes Zakia's picture. Nordland, who relates the episode with a sort of glee, seems unconcerned or simply uninterested in how the episode connects to a history of colonial subjugation, of disrespect for feminine realms, of the autonomy of the conquered woman. Nor, it seems, are his editors: the photographs are published by the *New York Times*, the incident recounted in great detail with little regret and much entitlement.

*

Brave white women and veiled others

The aesthetic of the veil as repressive—and the premise that giving it up signifies freedom while retention suggests a continued commitment to female repression—is inextricably tied to the history of colonialism and the concomitant emergence of the veil as a visible symbol of what needed to be eliminated from the societies of colonized people such that they, or specifically their women, could be "taught" feminism. This last facet, the veil or veiled spaces as the aesthetic of a lack of empowerment, becomes most prominent in the role white women have played in the veiling and unveiling of "other" colonized women.

As is the case of white men (the colonizing French or British), the history of white women situating themselves as the empowered, enlightened and lucky (against the misfortunes of black and brown women) has a long history. In her article "Cutting Across Imperial Feminisms," feminist scholar Basuli Deb[13] points to the photography done by imperial women from around the same time as Alloula's postcards from Algeria.[14] One of these, taken by the British explorer Freya Stark, who traveled widely in the Middle East in the 1930s, features a Kuwaiti woman in a black burqa, rendered diminutive against the wall of the buildings and the elongated shadows on them. In another photo taken by a lesser-known British photographer named

Marjorie Armstrong, Deb notes how the camera angle and perspective render the women into "a conglomeration of black," amounting to "a transformation of Arab women into still-life objects." In the absence of these silent native women speaking back, an enlightened epistemology is created, poised on an aesthetic in which "the burka is the ultimate yardstick of female oppression," whose measure justifies and legitimates both the colonial presence and colonial violence.

Nothing, it seems, has changed. If the white women of the colonial era presented themselves as explorers and archaeologists, Freya Stark and Gertrude Bell notable among them, their descendants are more often journalists or perhaps aid workers. For contemporary Western female journalists, the project of representing intimate spaces, such as the ones I inhabited growing up, is a reliable path to success. In her memoir *It's What I Do: A Photographer's Life of Love and War*, photographer Lynsey Addario[15] writes of how a male mentor advised her "to go to Afghanistan to photograph women living under the Taliban" in the first place. The success of her series *Women of Jihad* in the wake of 9/11 paved her path to the *Times* and a MacArthur "genius" grant.

Decades before Addario visited Afghanistan, former *New York Times* reporter Judith Miller made similar calculations when she became the first female chief of the Cairo bureau in 1983. Her arrival came not long after a class-action suit by female journalists at the *Times* forced the paper to open its reporting and editorial positions to women. Like Addario, Miller admits that she "sometimes profited from the virtual invisibility of women in the most restrictive Arab countries and used it to gain access to places from which men were barred." The gendered politics of Addario's own career—her goal of proving herself as a worthy war photographer, and her underscoring of the special access she has to the intimate female spaces of the Muslim world—are all political aspects of the Western woman's own fight against patriarchy. The "veiled" others are imagined relying on the intrepid courage of these women who imagine themselves (as did their forbears) engaged in bringing feminism and visibility to the lesser women of conquered lands.

*

A new look for the veil

As was visible from her performance piece that recorded the reactions of her peers to her voluntary veiling, artists like Shahzia Sikander[16] who are both Muslim and feminist have tried to complicate the simplistic aesthetic in which all veiled women are oppressed and backward victims of coercion, and unveiled women reveling in the display of their faces and bodies represent ever higher quotients of empowerment. Sikander's interventions are two-pronged. Even as her performance piece focuses on the Western obsession with the veil—while retaining the veiled woman as a silent and voiceless subject—the rest of her work focuses on questioning Muslim tradition and its erasure of female voices and representations.

Sikander trained in Lahore at the National College of Art, where she learned the long neglected art of traditional Mughal miniature painting. Few of her fellow students were interested in what was seen as a largely dated and dead art form. Sikander gave the form new meaning, her paintings playing with the traditional rules of form and content, inserting feminine figures and even self-portraits within the compositions. This remarkable reconfiguration, novel in mode of expression, challenged both local patriarchies and their long-standing practice of silencing and erasing women from history, and orientalist stereotypes that similarly imagined women as voiceless, incapable of artistic and independent expression.

Sikander is not alone. The work of Iranian-American artist Shirin Neshat was recently featured in a retrospective at the Hirshorn Museum in Washington D.C. The exhibition, titled Facing History,[17] takes on the complexities of an oppressive Iranian regime and a dismissive United States given to demonizing all Iranians and women caught in the middle. Neshat's work spans three periods in Iranian history. The first period begins with the 1953 ouster of Iran's first democratically elected prime minister, Mohammad Mossadeq, orchestrated in large part by the United States. The second, far better known for its binary optics of extremism and tyranny, is the 1979 Islamic Revolution that led to the overthrow of the shah and the ascent of Ayatollah Khomeini.

The final period is the most recent, the hopeful if limitedly successful Green Revolution, which saw scores of Iranian youth, particularly women, taking to the streets of Tehran and demanding democracy and freedom from oppression.

If the political distorts the real into caricatures that align with the political agendas of enemy making, the artistic can do the opposite: unearth and enhance the real as the beautiful. In this exhibition, photographs from Neshat's *Women of Allah* series are the strongest. In these portraits, the faces, eyes, and hands of the artist and other female subjects are transcribed with Persian poetry. This theme of transcription recurs in all three historical periods to which Neshat attends. Here the black-encased women of the past and the fresh-faced male and female youth of the Green Revolution address how the metaphorical Iranian-Muslim must appear to America and Americans: unintelligible and overwrought. The fact that this striated relationship can be and is, in Neshat's delicate recreation, one of attraction and beauty is a testament that artistic possibility can achieve what the political may find impossible—or at least improbable.

Neshat's most striking photographic compositions are from her *Women of Allah Series* (1993–1997), many of which feature women clad in full black veils and holding weapons. Images of women in black chadors clasping guns were a familiar part of the post-1979 Iranian Regime's project of reconstituting the understanding of women's empowerment, not as a Western-derived pursuit of gender equality, but rather as a literal wielding of destructive power to fight for basic rights. In Neshat's representation of ideas of segregation and militarization, guns and veils come together to represent the twin dangers a woman can pose, one of a palpable if veiled sexuality and the other of the literal bullet in the barrel.

In the years since Neshat created her iconic images of Iranian women, this competing idea of Muslim women's agency and empowerment has spread beyond Iran. The darkly clad weapon-wielding woman of Neshat's photograph, "Rebellious Silence" (1994), features a chador-clad woman holding a gun barrel upright against her face such that it bisects her body in half. This woman warrior stares directly at the camera, her gaze both distant and resolute. In the decades since "Rebellious Silence" was shot, the idea of the covered woman as warrior has begun to signify a competing conception of empowerment centered on gender segregation rather than parity. Its visible anti-Western and anti-imperialist points of reference are imagined as more authentic for Iranian women than one focused only on equality, on women being *like* men, or other simplistic parallels tying unveiling with freedom. Because the Islamist veiled and armed woman-warrior model is focused on complementarity instead of equality, it envisions the realms of men and women as separate but imbued with their own power structures in which women can rise to leadership.

Some legitimacy for this conception of gender relations has been supplied by the doubts feminist scholars like

Aysha Hidayatullah have expressed for the task of finding theological support for gender equality within Islamic theological texts. Power is hence being reconstructed and reconstituted: Neshat's women wield guns and supplicate at the same time; their veils do not stanch their sexuality; the female gaze looking back at the audience is bold and unflinching. Women in orthodox religious schools in Iran and beyond—in Islamabad, in Muslim ghettoes in France and Britain—now consume and sometimes adopt this alternative conception of the feminine, a premonition of which appeared in Neshat's *Women of Allah* series decades ago in images such as *Rebellious Silence* and "Faceless" (both works, 1994).[18] The latter also features a woman in chador, but now her gun is pointed at the viewer.

A veil is revealed then to be not just fabric but a partition and a boundary; transgressing it represents intrusion and domination. To put the veil back on, to retreat into feminine space, is a wish for reclamation.

5 SUBMISSIVE OR SUBVERSIVE

I was getting to the point where a courtroom no longer frightened me. I could eat a few bites before a hearing, I could make small talk with my client . . . my hands were not completely drenched in sweat. Armed with this almost confidence, I sat on the counsel's chair with my client. It was a divorce hearing, not the final one or the preliminary one, just one where we decided dates for future hearings and gave an update on the possibilities of mediation. My client was living in the domestic violence shelter where I worked; amicable settlements did not seem to be in the cards but the judge wanted us to try, and so we were there to say that we were.

Sometime after I had made my presentation before the judge, my attention wandered. I was still listening as the opposing counsel was talking about his client's work schedule, his dissatisfaction with the visitation arrangement that had been set up at a prior hearing. Suddenly I heard the judge say "Excuse me, Excuse me Counsel, could you trouble yourself to look at me." Stung and red-faced, I turned to look at the judge. He did not have anything in particular to say, he only wanted me to look at him while I was in the courtroom. It was disrespectful not to do so, he told me, and he had the authority to discipline me if I did not comply. I did comply, looked at him for the remaining twenty minutes of the hearing and for each one that followed.

On January 19, 2010, a woman named Aafia Siddiqui was led into a Federal courthouse in Manhattan. She wore a full-face veil. A little over two years before, Siddiqui had been charged with a torrent of offenses, including but not limited to the attempted murder of US officials and servicemen. The complaint listing the charges was initially sealed and it was not until Siddiqui had been extradited from Afghanistan, where the incident supposedly took place, that these charges were even known.

The day leading up to the first day of the trial had also been tumultuous, the heated exchanges between Siddiqui and Judge Berman focusing on, among other things, whether Siddiqui had to consent to being strip-searched every morning before she could come into the courtroom. According to the trial transcript, Berman tried to press Siddiqui into waiving her right to be present in the courtroom because she insisted that she did not want to undergo a strip search. Siddiqui, either obstinate or not understanding, refused to waive her right to be physically present and to watch the proceedings from the closed circuit television camera in her holding cell. It went on for a while.

On the first day of trial, however, Siddiqui is present in the New York courtroom not far from where the 9/11 attackers brought down the Twin Towers. As sketches from the courtroom from that day (no television cameras were allowed) reveal, Siddiqui wore a beige colored veil that concealed everything but her eyes. The jurors would never actually see her. They would, however, hear her. When she took the stand nine days into the trial as part of the defense case, Siddiqui insisted that the charges against her were false, emphasizing the fact that she is a petite woman and rejecting the idea that she could grab an M-6 rifle. "That is the biggest lie that I am forced to smile under my scarf," Siddiqui told the jury.[1]

That was not the only time that the jury heard Siddiqui's voice. Numerous times during the trial, she interrupted the judge or lawyers or a witness that was speaking, accusing them of lying or presenting their own views. Each time the judge censured her, choosing in later instances to have her taken back to the holding cell where she could see what was happening on closed circuit television. These outbursts by a fully veiled woman became part of the prosecution's closing arguments. A defendant as feisty and spirited as the one interrupting everyone, it was said, would be just as capable of grabbing a gun and attempting to shoot soldiers. The jury deliberated for three days, considering the charges against a woman they had never seen face to face. They found her guilty on all counts.

*

Courts and compliance

Aafia Siddiqui is currently serving her eighty-six-year sentence at Carswell Federal Prison in Texas. Most of America has forgotten about this MIT-educated neuroscientist who was also the very first full-veiled woman to be tried and convicted on attempted murder charges in the United States. Others, however, have not forgotten. In a letter to the parents of kidnapped journalist James Foley, the Islamic State demanded her release as one of the conditions for releasing their son. None of the conditions were met, of course, and Foley was beheaded, the grisly video of the killing circulated widely and around the world.

I have long been interested in Siddiqui's case. Why would a woman as seemingly intelligent as Siddiqui choose to wear a full-face veil in a Manhattan courtroom? Earlier photographs of Siddiqui show that she did not always wear a veil, and often not even a headscarf. In a newsreel from the summer of 2008, when Siddiqui and her son were found wandering the streets of Ghazni, Afghanistan, Siddiqui wears a traditional chador; she covers her face not with a full-face veil but just the edge of her chador, a tactic used by many Pakistani and Afghan women if they find themselves surrounded by men. In the video, Siddiqui is surrounded by men; goaded by the camera, her voice is small, barely audible. She is asking to be left alone.

Would a woman interested in being free deliberately choose to wear a veil before a Manhattan jury? No one considered this question during Siddiqui's trial. The judge did consider whether Siddiqui was mentally competent to stand trial. On November 17, 2008, two months after she had been extradited from Afghanistan to the United States, Judge Berman—the same judge who would ultimately preside over Siddiqui's trial—sent an order to the lawyers in the case. In that order, Berman ruled that based on the results of a court-ordered psychological evaluation, Siddiqui was not fit to stand trial. Specifically, she could not understand the nature and consequences of the court proceedings and could not assist in the preparation of her own defense.

By July 2009 he had changed his mind. A hearing was held that month in which the issue of her competency was considered again. The prosecution had by now acquired a new forensic psychologist from the military to conduct the evaluation. This new expert found that Siddiqui was just pretending to be crazy and was a "malingerer," not someone with actual psychiatric illness. In turn, the defense presented their own psychological evaluation, its results showing that Siddiqui was delusional and psychiatrically unstable. The outbursts at pre-trial hearings were presented as evidence that Siddiqui was not fit to stand trial. Judge Berman, however, made his own determination regarding what the outbursts meant. Siddiqui was quiet until the prosecution pointed out that she was very compliant, after which she stepped up her outbursts. That evidence, held Berman, was sufficient to prove that she was, after all, competent to stand trial.

Berman's ruling reflects warring tensions, the vexing choice between conceptualizing this veiled woman as a madwoman, acting and behaving bizarrely and often not in her own interest, or as a terrorist pretending to be crazy so that she would not have to stand trial. While these are abstract questions, the veil covering all of Siddiqui's face cannot be considered incidental to them. It could even be argued that Siddiqui's refusal to face those present in the courtroom and her preoccupation with being strip-searched point to the significance of this physical object—the veil—in constructing her identity before the judge and jury.

The tension between considering whether Siddiqui was crazy or sinister also points also to how the War on Terror attempts to transform the fully veiled woman from submissive to terrorist. Siddiqui's trial, the presentation of and acceptance of the "malingerer" as an explanation of her bizarre behavior, reflects in literal terms this metaphoric tension, the need to explain away the submissive to make room for the subversive. The fully veiled Muslim woman, once imagined as singularly exotic and repressed, an emblem of the harem of old, ripe with forbidden sexual possibility, did not fit into rhetoric of the War on Terror. That War could no longer be based simply on the demonization of the Muslim man; it required an extension of suspicion to the Muslim woman, particularly the Muslim woman who was not willing to do away with the veil. The details of Siddiqui's trial can be dissected and debated, but there is no doubt about the fact that Siddiqui insisted on wearing a full-face veil.

The veil as security threat

The Western proclivity toward redefining the fully veiled woman as subversive rather than submissive can also be traced to the increased Western need to control the aesthetics of public spaces. Early versions of burka bans met with resistance from supporters of multiculturalism because of their imposition of one set of values on religious minority women. France's 2004 ban on the headscarf, for instance, added at least symbolically to its popularity as a political symbol of resistance against an overreaching state. This reality, recurrent in other contexts where aspects of Islamic practice faced bans, led to the development of a counter-narrative where it was the state that was labeled coercive.

The security narrative that paints the full-face veil as subversive and hence deserving of a ban is likely to be much more successful. Terrorist attacks in several European countries (even though none have been conducted by women wearing full-face veils) created a fertile ground for these restrictions. The aesthetic aversion to the veil (as to the minaret) as an unwelcome modifier of the European landscape, its colonizer if you will, could now be mixed inextricably with the fear of terrorism. This result is a transformation of the fully veiled woman from the hapless subject requiring Western rescue to the subversive terrorist requiring imprisonment.

This narrative has been bolstered by the industry of terror analysts and experts that has emerged in the years since 9/11.

Increasingly, female terror experts have chosen to focus on female jihadis, using what little data is available to support the premise that this particular category of terrorist is one that poses a serious threat and has policy implications. "Cruel Intentions: Female Jihadists in America" is the title of one recent report[2] that is part of the discursive project proving that Muslim women are not submissive but subversive. Its author, a researcher named Audrey Alexander, eagerly tells readers at the very outset that previous beliefs in Muslim women's lack of agency are "historic distortions" that have led contemporary research to "overlook or diminish" their potential for subversion.

For the remainder of the report Alexander, who is a Research Fellow at George Washington University's Program on Extremism, utilizes a vocabulary that underscores just how dangerous these historic distortions are when it comes to keeping Westerners safe. Again and again, she uses words like "notable uptick," "increase," "wave," and "ever-expanding" to describe the magnitude of the threat. Her own numbers, however, do not substantiate these descriptions; Alexander's data consist of only twenty-five cases that have emerged in the five-year period between 2011 and 2016, a number she describes as a "wealth of data."

Next, Alexander handily conjures a typology that classifies female jihadists into one of three categories: plotters, supporters, and travelers. As broad and arbitrary as they are, these categories could be tweaked to include just about any visibly (and "visibly" increasingly means *veiled*) Muslim women. She admits this fact herself, telling us how the "supporter" "category" has "a low threshold of participation," sometimes amounting to nothing more than social media activity. The import of this can be missed by those within and beyond the United States who are not aware of the already hawkish interpretation adopted by US courts of the Material Support for Terrorism statute.[3] Recent court decisions have held that even accidental dissemination of material, without any knowledge of its content or intent of actual material support, is sufficient for a conviction. What Alexander wants is an even more draconian interpretation, one in which an accidental "like" or share on social media, or a Facebook friend-of-a-friend involved in jihadist activity, can lead to a decades-long prison sentence.

Colonialism thrived because it rested on its own epistemology, theories of knowledge that painted brown and black peoples of the world as inferior, requiring civilization and taming by enlightened and ever-benevolent Westerners. In that era, depicting Muslim women as suffering bore the advantage of presenting Muslim men as not simply racially and intellectually inferior but also morally flawed, unable to respect their own. Since colonialism's field of operation was overseas instead of at home, this justified intervention. In this age of terror, the battle is at home and the old paradigm yields no strategic dividends. Western Muslim women's visible expressions of agency, manifested by their demands to decide for themselves how they wish to practice their faith or whether or not they wish to veil, require a new paradigm that justifies their exclusion, ostracism, and even imprisonment. The emerging "research," much of which consists of similarly flimsy and poorly articulated exhortations pointing to their secret subversion, does just that. Curbs on the civil liberties of Muslim women can thus be easily justified, their treatment as suspects now a required precaution enacted to protect society from their nefarious proclivities

Given all of this, the real contribution made by a report like "Cruel Intentions"[4] is that its author recognizes that a re-imagining of the Muslim woman, her transition from pitiable submissive to suspicious subversive, poses an epistemological challenge. Allotting too much agency to Muslim women threatens to dislodge the enduring arrangement of Western feminism, for which the Muslim woman has been the lesser sister. Alexander devises a clever solution: female jihadists are no rebels; it is instead their propensity for "nurturing and sustenance" that is crucial to their diabolical ability to dupe. The kindly Muslim mom, the shy Muslim wife, probably any Muslim woman can effortlessly "transcend" such roles, morphing into the violent, ruthless, and extremely dangerous female jihadist. In the guise of a research report, a tempting logic of widespread suspicion is offered up to Westerners who care to consider it, one that dictates that Muslim women are *all* in possession of cruel intentions, each of them secretly marching toward jihad, guilty or not but never ever innocent

This epistemological shift is particularly relevant in relation to the veil. The physical act of wearing a full-face veil, a visible symbol of being Muslim, is now converted into an epistemological metaphor. Within its dimensions, all Muslim women are veiled—true identities as plotters, supporters, or travelers, obscured by the seemingly benign front that Western culture and its "historic" distortions has applied to them. The unveiling that is required, then, is not simply the literal one of old, the project of colonial excursion eager to penetrate the harem, but one that requires getting into the heads and lives of these women for the greater good of protecting the world from them.

*

Acknowledgment of the political value of the veil as object is not limited to the Western world. When the Taliban came into power in Afghanistan and then later in parts of Pakistan, one of the first things they did was to require women to wear a full-face veil; violators were publicly disciplined. Similarly and more recently, when the Islamic State seized power in parts of Iraq and Syria, one of their first edicts was to require all women to wear the full veil. To enforce this ruling, an all-women vice squad called "Al-Khansaa Brigade" was mobilized. Their job was to catch, detain, and punish women who were violating the ban even in small ways: too much of their faces, wisps of hair, flashy socks could catch attention and result in being disciplined and punished. It has been a useful strategy, employing women to correct other women—hand some women weapons and flog others.

The usual Western commentary on the extremist enforcement of the full-face veil has centered on the implementation of a fringe version of orthodox Islam that imagined the invisibility of women as a requirement. This same line of argument is accepted by Muslims trying to combat extremist propaganda and who focus on the fact that the full-face veil is not theologically required. Both miss the point. The Taliban enforcement of the veil, while literally justified as Islamic, is more likely to be motivated by the need for an instant transformation of public space that also emerges from the ban. The sudden elimination of women, or their relegation to a garment that makes them difficult to identify, is centrally rooted in underscoring how everyday life and familiar context have both changed. It is a powerful tool to establish the authority of the new men in charge.

It is also true that this aesthetic transformation wrought by militant organizations exists in current dialogue on fear of the burka in the West. The increasing emphasis on banning the full-face veil by Western states because of security concerns is related to militant groups seeking in turn to bolster the visible numbers of women in burkas. If, as Westerners are told to believe, all fully veiled women are secretly subversive, then it follows that showing their large numbers suggests an army in waiting.

This is not to say that the image of a woman clad all in black is entirely meant for Western consumption. Muslim audiences are just as susceptible to the projections of power and transformation that are suggested by full-veiled women. One instance of this took place in 2007 in Pakistan. In June of that year, several girls from Jamiah Hafsa,[5] an all-female religious seminary located in Islamabad, got into a car after the last prayers of the day had concluded and the capital city settled in for the night. The women, dressed in black from head to toe, were on a mission. Through Islamabad's quiet nighttime streets, they drove to a massage parlor, whose location they had stalked out weeks earlier, and rang the bell. When the door opened, they saw twenty-five Chinese women dressed only in their underwear and lounging on couches. Faced with the black-clad Jamiah Hafsa women, the occupants scattered, most trying to hide in the more remote rooms of the house. Five of them were unable to hide and were apprehended by the girls from the madrasah, who wrapped them up in shawls for modesty and took them back to Jamiah Hafsa.

The kidnapped women remained at the madrasah for more than twenty-four hours, during which the flustered government of General Pervez Musharraf tried to appease irate Chinese officials. The act was the boldest of a campaign of moral vigilantism in which the girls of Jamiah Hafsa had been engaged for months—an effort, they stated, in response to the failure of the Pakistani government to safeguard the moral values of the society. To register their protest, the Jamiah Hafsa women, many toting large bamboo sticks known as *lathis*, often stood en masse on the street outside the institution. Months earlier, they had also occupied and taken over an adjoining children's library, run by the government, to further taunt the Pakistani state. Because the library was a public space, its occupation represented, in a very visible way, the women's ability to take away something from the public as well the state, right in Pakistan's capital city. The fact that it was a children's library said even more: that the cultivation of the future generation belonged not to the government of Pakistan, but to the women of Jamiah Hafsa. The acts of the Jamiah Hafsa women set off a siege of the adjoining Red Mosque that lasted several months and ended with a storming of the compound by the Pakistani military, a decision that is credited for having instigated the eventual collapse of the Musharraf government later that same year. One leader, Abdul Rasheed Ghazi, was killed in the military operation along with seventy-two other people. Ghazi's older brother, Abdul Aziz, was apprehended attempting to leave the besieged compound wearing a woman's burka.

The women of Jamiah Hafsa—young, militant, and organized—demonstrated the ability of Islamist movements to penetrate women's lives and spur them to political action. The Islamist women of Jamiah Hafsa had employed a particular recipe for success. Cultural norms in Pakistan keep women in the private sphere by imposing costs on families that risk their honor by exposing their women to the vagaries of public life in education or employment. Allied with gender, religion became a counter argument to culture, and the objections of fathers and brothers could be overcome, because in this case the women's leaving the private sphere was part of accomplishing their divine duty. As activists, they were doing the work of bringing about a more Islamic society, where the modesty of women and their role as mothers of the *ummah* (worldwide Islamic community) would be respected.

Thus envisioned, they would be warriors, a role permitted by faith, if not by the patriarchal culture that surrounded them. In 2014, not long after fighters from the Islamic State declared the formation of the Islamic Caliphate, the women of Jamiah Hafsa, still fully veiled, recorded a YouTube video. In it, they declared their fealty to Abu Bakar Al Baghdadi, the self-proclaimed Caliph of the Islamic State.

While some fully veiled women sporting black burkas (like the women of Jamiah Hafsa) may have militant sympathies, many others wear them for the freedom it offers from social mores and from being identified. Anonymity has its own power, particularly in a society where what is seen in public is held to be true and to have moral import; conversely, what is unseen and unknown does not. This dichotomy means that the burka offers cover for acts that may be considered immoral in a particular society. I saw one example of this, five years after the Jamia Hafsa incident. Around the end of January 2012, Maya Khan, the host of a popular morning show called *Mornings with Maya*, decided to take a camera crew into a Karachi park. The objective was to shame publicly the many couples that have begun to use public parks for dates and trysts. Prior to taking on the unaware lovers, Maya Khan, who herself wears a traditional shalwar kameez and does not cover her hair, interviewed a number of women, each of whom vehemently condemned the colonization of public space by these errant couples. On that day, as viewers across Pakistan watched, Khan, flanked by a small coterie of supporters and her camera crew, marched into a public park. On seeing the cameras, several couples fled, but one or two were cornered. The men appeared indignant, and the women, all of whom were in burkas, simply pulled down their niqabs before they could be exposed.

This spectacle set off a spirited debate, which exposed the ambiguous translation both of women wearing the veil and of the transformation of public space in Pakistan. Central to the exposé was the ambiguity of the fully veiled woman. Maya Khan's actions had in a sense subverted the example of the women of Jamiah Hafsa. In that situation, the fully veiled women had been the enforcers of morality. On Maya Khan's show the burka was exposed as a convenient cover for doing things that would have met the censure of Pakistani conservatives who frown on men and women dating. It also transformed the public space in which the couples were meeting into a place where private conversations could take place because one of the people engaged in them could not be identified.

*

Being seen, being watched, and being veiled

Western people have been less interested in considering these ambiguities of the veil. The refusal of the veiled woman to be visible is poised against the security imperatives delineated by the Western state to protect its citizens. The instruments of allotting particular identities, the photographing and fingerprinting that occurs at European and American borders to consider eligibility for admission, impose a certain kind of visibility on veiled women. No exception or rebellion is permissible against this requirement. In this new land, where they have arrived, identity must be constructed according to these postulates and categories. For those who have left bereft economic conditions or war or refugee camps, there is no choice but to accede.

Once admitted, however, these totems of identity do not confer belonging. Female Muslim immigrants, particularly in European countries like France and Switzerland and other places that have instituted a ban on the full-face veil, find themselves relegated to ghettoes and immigrant enclaves. Even as requirements are imposed on the terms on which they are accepted, the acceptance of these terms does not confer a concomitant welcome into European public culture, which continues to be defined by Christian and post-enlightenment values—reflecting little of the concerns or ideas of those who have made Europe their home in the past fifty years. The cataloging, fingerprinting, and surveillance of immigrant exists as a means of assessing danger, not constructing dialogue.

Far from the West, similar surveillance is conducted using technology. Drones fly over Somalia, Iraq, Afghanistan, and Pakistan, creating continual surveillance of all below. The veil as object is feeble against the omniscience of the drone, its perpetual camera, its constant vigilance. Privacy is annihilated and in its place there is a sort of collective blame. As many drone operators have revealed, the search is for patterns, whose identification is a precursor to the strike, which is a precursor to destruction. Women are not normally targeted, but if they happen to be in the strike radius determined to hold a militant, their killing is justified. With only bits and pieces of information regarding the aftermath of strikes, casualty reports are not forthcoming, and numbers and names of the dead even less so. While actual death may or may not be dealt by a drone, the death of privacy is certain. If the veil ban requires and institutes a certain aesthetic in the European public sphere touting the lack of identification and the cover of anonymity as part of the rationale requiring its imposition, it imposes the opposite on the areas patrolled by drones. In those places, individuality and identity is poised on the scant evidence provided by patterns, blame imposed via geography rather than culpability.

With the veiled woman reconstructed as the subversive, the potential or actual terrorist, the surveillance regimes of Western states are deemed justified. The motivation for getting into the heads of certain types of people, Muslims and immigrants, particularly those who in their adoption of the veil attempt to resist surveillance are now believed to *require* such sorts of monitoring. The veil is hence elevated in the Western imagination as the physical and visible symbol of subterfuge on a much larger scale and to all adherents of an entire faith. All of them, veiled or unveiled, are complicit in a conspiracy against the West, livid at Western largesse, uninterested in Western freedoms. Watching them imposing visibility by bans or drones is an imperative, and any resistance at all a certain indication of guilt.

EPILOGUE

I began writing this meditation on the veil long before the American election season had reached a fever pitch, before it seemed likely that Donald Trump would be the Republican nominee and long before it seemed he would win the US Presidential Election. I was in the midst of writing it when on December 7, 2015, Trump announced that he would be instituting a "Muslim ban."[1] His supporters shouted anti-Muslim slogans at his rallies and at least one was filmed yelling "Death to Muslims." Around the country, women who wore headscarves were taunted and attacked: "Go back where you came from," the assailants yelled. Others were not satisfied with only verbal threats—they pulled at their headscarves, shoved their bodies. The Muslim veil has now become a target that must be attacked to insure the welfare of the country, its elimination and the banishment of its wearers crucial and necessary to "Make America Great Again."

Donald Trump did not wait long to deliver on his promise of a Muslim ban. Less than a month into his term, he signed an Executive Order that banned anyone from seven Muslim countries from traveling to the United States, banned all refugees for ninety days, and all Syrian refugees for an indefinite period. Soon after he signed the order, President Trump appeared on the Christian Broadcasting Network and said that while Muslim refugees had been banned, Christian refugees would be given preference toward resettling in the United States. Not long before the actual order was signed, former New York City mayor Rudy Giuliani had appeared in a televised interview saying that he and others had been tasked with casting the Muslim ban in language that would meet legal criteria (and appear not to target Muslims).

The targets of the ban are, of course, Muslims—and given that the veil, whether it is a full- or half-face veil or a headscarf, is one of the most visible symbols of Muslim identity— Trump's Muslim ban has situated it at the center of the venomous politics of Trump's America. If Trump supporters had been virulent and aggressive before, the institution of the ban, which has been temporarily held in abeyance by a court-ordered injunction, they have since been emboldened and even legitimized by the institution of the ban. Soon, demanding the removal of veils and headscarves and subjecting wearers to aggressive and intrusive scrutiny will be elevated to a national security requirement. If the National Security team is led by those who believe that all Muslims are terrorists, then women who avow their Muslim identity by wearing a headscarf are most certainly terrorist suspects.

A little over a week after the first travel ban was enjoined by a judge (and the next one not yet put into place), I traveled to Europe. On my way back at the Paris airport, I stood in line to have my passport and documents checked a second time. A Muslim woman who wore a headscarf was a few steps ahead of me. We both watched as an olive-skinned man, who may or may not have been Muslim, was searched by agents, required to remove a sweater vest, a jacket, a scarf, as a crowd of at least a hundred watched. When it was her turn to walk past the table (the un-suspicious are permitted to board without being stopped) the woman, neat and prim in her headscarf, simply walked up to the desk herself and offered up her belongings.

I could not then decide if this was an act of dignity or defeat; it was however an emblem of change. Latent prejudice instigated by a religious symbol has always been a part of American, and perhaps any, society. There is a difference, however, when that lurking prejudice is justified by legal imprimatur, elevated to a virtue signifying love of country, of putting "America First." All of what I have written in previous chapters must thus be considered with this new reality in mind, a reality that has resurrected what is darkest and ugly, but now insists on its comely beauty. The veil as object appears now accompanied and offset by other veils: the veils of ignorance and bigotry, the veils of prejudice and hatred, of xenophobia and racism. These veils cannot be seen as easily as the veil that is the subject of this book, but they enable their own subterfuge, take from all those caught in their folds the ability to see.

NOTES

Chapter 2

1 See Amina Wadud, *Quran and Women* (New York: Oxford University Press, 1993); Jonathan Brown, *Misquoting Muhammad: The Challenge and Choices of Interpreting the Prophet's Legacy* (London: Oneworld Publications, 2014).

2 See http://worldhijabday.com/about-us/ (last accessed April 17, 2017).

3 Ibid.

Chapter 3

1 See http://www.independent.co.uk/news/uk/home-news/ beyond-the-veil-what-happened-after-rebekah-dawson- refused-to-take-her-niqab-off-in-court-9244409.html (last accessed on April 17, 2014).

2 See R. v. N.S., [2012] 3 S.C.R. 726, which can be viewed at https://scc-csc.lexum.com/scc-csc/scc-csc/en/item/12779/ index.do?r=AAAAAQAMMyBTLkMuUi4gNzI2AQ (last accessed on April 17, 2017).

3   See http://www.apa.org/pubs/journals/releases/lhb-
    lhb0000189.pdf (last accessed on April 17, 2017).

4   See http://www.telegraph.co.uk/news/2016/07/07/burka-ban-
    for-muslims-enforced-in-switzerland-with-fines-of-up-t/ (last
    accessed on April 17, 2017).

5   Todd H. Green, "The Resistance to Minarets in Europe,"
    J Church State 52, no. 4 (2010): 619–643, which can
    be viewed at https://academic.oup.com/jcs/article-
    abstract/52/4/619/870913/The-Resistance-to-Minarets-in-
    Europe?redirectedFrom=fulltext (last accessed on April 17,
    2017).

6   See http://www.independent.co.uk/news/world/africa/egypt-
    drafts-bill-to-ban-niqab-veil-in-public-places-a6920701.html
    (last accessed on April 17, 2017).

7   See http://www.aljazeera.com/news/2017/01/reports-
    morocco-bans-production-sale-burqa-170110140716164.html
    (last accessed on April 17, 2017).

Chapter 4

1   See http://www.chicagoreader.com/chicago/on-exhibit-
    shahzia-sikander-makes-herself-clear/Content?oid=895731
    (last accessed April 17, 2017).

2   See https://www.c-span.org/video/?c4645885/rep-carolyn-
    maloney-wears-burka-house-floor (last accessed April 17, 2017).

3   See http://articles.latimes.com/2001/nov/18/news/mn-5602
    (last accessed April 17, 2017).

4   http://www.feminist.org/news/pressstory.asp?id=6449 (last
    accessed April 17, 2017).

5 See http://www.csun.edu/~sm60012/GRCS-Files/Readings/
   Russo-Feminist_Majority.pdf (last accessed April 17, 2017).

6 See https://atwar.blogs.nytimes.com/2011/05/05/my-first-
   afghan-burqa/?_r=0 (last accessed April 17, 2017).

7 See http://www.informit.com/articles/article.aspx?p=27303
   (last accessed April 17, 2017).

8 Malek Alloula, *The Colonial Harem* (Minneapolis: University
   of Minnesota Press, 1986).

9 See http://www.skny.com/attachment/
   en/56d5695ecfaf342a038b4568/Press/
   580b84288cdb501361a7ca06 (last accessed April 17, 2017).

10 Malek Alloula, *The Colonial Harem* (Minneapolis: University
   of Minnesota Press, 1986).

11 *National Geographic*, June 1985.

12 Rod Nordland, *The Lovers: Afghanistan's Romeo and Juliet, the
   True Story of How They Defied Their Families and Escaped an
   Honor Killing* (Harper Collins, 2016).

13 Basuli Deb. "Cutting across Imperial Feminisms toward
   Transnational Feminist Solidarities." *Meridians* 13, no. 2
   (2016): 164–88. doi:10.2979/meridians.13.2.09.

14 Malek Alloula, *The Colonial Harem* (Minneapolis: University
   of Minnesota Press, 1986).

15 Lynsey Addario, *It's What I Do: A Photographer's Life of Love
   and War* (New York: Penguin 2015).

16 See http://www.chicagoreader.com/chicago/on-exhibit-
   shahzia-sikander-makes-herself-clear/Content?oid=895731
   (last accessed April 17, 2017).

17 See https://hirshhorn.si.edu/collection/shirin-neshat/ (last
   accessed April 17, 2017).

18 See https://www.khanacademy.org/humanities/ap-art-history/global-contemporary/a/neshat-rebellious (last accessed April 17, 2017).

Chapter 5

1 Trial transcript.

2 See https://cchs.gwu.edu/sites/cchs.gwu.edu/files/downloads/Female%20Jihadists%20in%20America.pdf (last accessed April 17, 2017).

3 See http://www.cjr.org/tow_center_reports/hate_terrorism_trump_election_social_media_american_muslims.php#hate-crimes-muslims (last accessed April 17, 2017).

4 See https://cchs.gwu.edu/sites/cchs.gwu.edu/files/downloads/Female%20Jihadists%20in%20America.pdf (last accessed April 17, 2017).

5 See https://www.dissentmagazine.org/article/pakistani-conundrum-public-private-and-female (last accessed April 17, 2017).

Epilogue

1 See http://www.cnn.com/2015/12/07/politics/donald-trump-muslim-ban-immigration/ (last accessed April 17, 2017).

INDEX